Geography Crafts for Kids

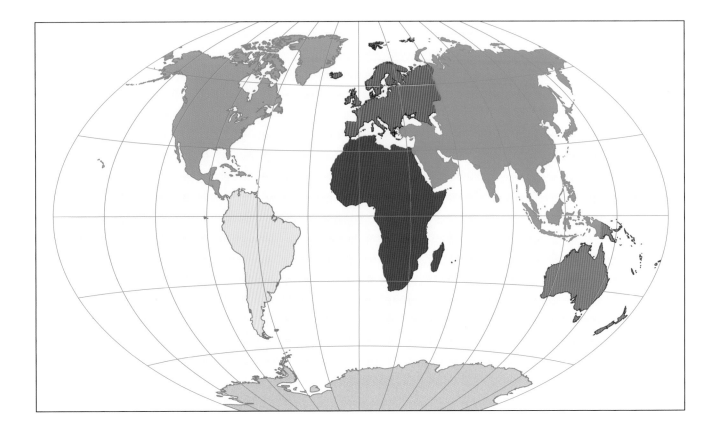

Geography Crafts for Kids

50 Cool Projects & Activities for Exploring the World

JOE RHATIGAN & HEATHER SMITH

LARK BOOKS
A Division of Sterling Publishing Co., Inc.
New York

To Kayleigh and Evan,
whose world explorations have
made me curious again.
— J. R.

I dedicate this book to
Linda Smith for passing on her
itchy feet and encouraging
the adventures they
take me on.
— H. S.

Art Director: Celia Naranjo
Cover Design: Barbara Zaretsky
Photography: Evan Bracken and Richard Hasselberg
Illustrations: Orrin Lundren
Editorial Assistance: Rain Newcomb, Nathalie Mornu, and Veronika Alice Gunter

Library of Congress Cataloging-in-Publication Data

Rhatigan, Joe.
    Geography crafts for kids : 50 cool projects & activities for exploring
the world / Joe Rhatigan and Heather Smith.— 1st ed.
      p. cm.
    ISBN 1-57990-196-4
    1. Geography—Study and teaching (Elementary)—Activity programs. I. Smith, Heather, 1974-
    II. Title.

    G75 .R44 2002
    372.89'1044—dc21

2001038649

10 9 8 7 6 5 4 3 2 1
First Edition

Published by Lark Books, a division of
Sterling Publishing Co., Inc.
387 Park Avenue South
New York, N.Y. 10016

© 2002, Lark Books

Distributed in Canada by Sterling Publishing,
c/o Canadian Manda Group, One Atlantic Ave., Suite 105
Toronto, Ontario, Canada M6K 3E7

Distributed in the U.K. by:
Guild of Master Craftsman Publications Ltd.
Castle Place, 166 High Street, Lewes, East Sussex, England
BN7 1XU
Tel: (+ 44) 1273 477374
Fax: (+ 44) 1273 478606
Email: pubs@thegmcgroup.com
Web: www.gmcpublications.com

Distributed in Australia by Capricorn Link (Australia) Pty Ltd., P.O. Box 704, Windsor, NSW 2756 Australia

If you have questions or comments about this book, please contact:
Lark Books
67 Broadway
Asheville, NC 28801
(828) 253-9730

Printed in Hong Kong

ISBN: 1-57990-196-4

CONTENTS

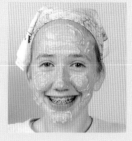

NOTE: The AS icon you'll see at the top of some project pages means that you'll need an adult to help you with the project.

YOU ARE H

NOW WHAT?

Big question, eh? I mean, here you are, one person in a room in a home on a street in a neighborhood in a town, city, village, hamlet, or farmstead in a state, province, or territory in a country on a continent in a hemisphere all on this large rock that spins around an even bigger ball of burning gas located at the tail end of the Milky Way galaxy, which is one of who knows how many galaxies in the universe, and, and...where were we? Oh yes, now what? That's the question that starts us on this fabulous journey known as geography.

There's no one definition of geography, though if we were to give it a shot, we'd say geography is the where, why, who, what, and when of all things related to Earth and the life-forms that call Earth home. Geography can tell you why you're right where you are right now and how you got there. It explores why your ancestors settled where they did, why your parents moved to the home you live in, and why you're reading a book in the United States, Canada, Australia, New Zealand, England, or elsewhere, that was written in the United States (in a small city in North Carolina, in an office without any windows), printed in Hong Kong from paper and ink manufactured in Japan, that got shipped to a warehouse in New Jersey (U.S.A.).

Geography is the air you breathe, the clothes you wear, the roads you travel. It snoops around, explores, and starts finding answers. And it doesn't stop there. It also solves the world's mysteries, checks out what old, dusty people did on Earth long ago, and how what they did affects you. It's maps and charts, navigation and discovery, problems and solutions.

Finally, geography declares that you are one of 6,200,000,000 people on this planet, and yet instead of making you feel insignificant, geography lets you in on one of the biggest secrets of all: Not only does Earth affect you, but you, even just little old you all by yourself, affect Earth. It's an astounding thought. It's like going into the past in a time machine and telling your great-great grandmother not to marry your great-great grandfather. You'd change everything. Well, you're changing the world right now, without a time machine, by simply breathing.

This isn't a textbook—there's no memorizing rivers or towns, and who cares if you can't remember the difference between an isthmus and a peninsula or a gulf and a bay. This book also doesn't pretend to cover everything that geography has to offer—even textbooks couldn't do that—but we're here to show off a lot of cool things to do and make, and the only thing that ties all this stuff together is geography.

The five chapters in this book all help define and explore different aspects of geography. Chapter One investigates how early explorers and geographers learned about, measured, and traveled the Earth, and gives you a head start on becoming a world explorer. No geography book is complete without lots of maps, so we've dedicated Chapter Two to the geographer's best friend: the map. Chapter Three explores world cultures and how even though the people of the world look, talk, and act differently, there are also a lot of similarities. Chapter Four delves into how Earth's weather, climate, landscape, and more affect human life and development, while Chapter Five shows how humans affect Earth.

One final thought: You may think Earth has pretty much been completely discovered, explored, and mapped. Well, that's what people thought 500 years ago, and little did they know what lay ahead of them!

Chapter 1

Where in the World Are You?

YOU'RE LOST...DESPERATELY LOST. Your mom told your dad to turn left at the next intersection, but he turned right instead, and now, by the time you get to your dream beach vacation, it'll be time to turn around and go back home (at least that's what it feels like)! Even in this day of computer-generated directions, incredibly accurate maps, and global positioning devices that can pinpoint where you are to within 30 feet (9 m), we still get lost. And sure, you may lose some quality time at the ocean, but you know you'll get there as soon as your dad breaks down, stops driving around, and asks for some directions. Early explorers,

however, didn't have that sense of security. They had a few maps and some crude instruments to help them get around (either by foot or by ship), but if they went for more than a day or so without seeing the sun or the stars, there could be big trouble. It was risky business being an explorer back then, and these next several projects and activities give you a chance to walk around in the great and not-so-great explorers' shoes and to experience what it must have been like to go where no one you know had ever been. We've also included some fun projects that will help turn you into a world explorer in no time at all!

Up until only a few hundred years ago, the main focus of geographers was simply figuring out where places were, which is not such an easy thing on a spherical planet. And even though our ancestors weren't very good at knowing where they were, that didn't stop them from exploring. In order not to become completely lost out on the seas, mariners had to rely on some pretty crude instruments simply to tell them their latitude. (Until the 18th century, navigators couldn't find their longitude at sea at all!)

The astrolabe was originally used to determine the movements and positions of stars, but then somebody got the bright idea to try using it on a ship. And it worked! Okay, it worked well enough so that sailors sort of knew kind of where they were going. Create your own astrolabe and check out the information on latitude and longitude on page 15.

WHAT YOU NEED

- Piece of corrugated cardboard, 7 x 7 inches (17.8 x 17.8 cm)
- Round lid or something to draw a circle with a 6-inch (15.2 cm) diameter
- Pencil
- Scissors or craft knife
- Round lid or something to draw a circle with a 4-inch (10.2 cm) diameter
- Awl or nail
- Hex bolt with wing nut, 1/4 x 1 inch (6 mm x 2.5 cm)
- Ruler
- Protractor
- Acrylic paints, including metallic gold
- Paintbrush
- Black, fine-point, permanent marker
- Piece of wood, 5 x 1 x 1/2 inch (12.7 x 2.5 x 1.3 cm)
- Drill, with a bit slightly larger than the bolt
- 2 flat washers that fit around the bolt
- Plastic drinking straw
- Scissors
- 2 long, straight pins
- Piece of heavy thread or string, 20 inches (50.8 cm) long
- 2 nuts to use as weights

WHAT YOU DO

1. Make the dial by tracing a 6-inch (15.2 cm) circle on the piece of cardboard. Cut the circle out with the scissors.

2. Center the lid for the 4-inch (10.2 cm) circle on the circle you just cut, and trace this smaller circle (figure 1 on page 14).

3. Use the awl or nail to poke a hole through the exact center of the circle. Enlarge the hole by turning the awl until the bolt slides through the hole.

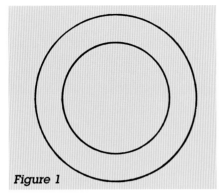

Figure 1

4. Use the ruler to help draw a straight line going from one edge of the cardboard circle to the other across the center hole. Label both ends of this line "0." Set the protractor on this line, with the center of the protractor over the center of the hole in the middle of the circle (figure 2).

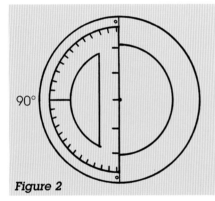

90°

Figure 2

5. The protractor is divided into numbered sections, beginning with 0 and going to 180, (straight up is 90°). Mark the place on the outer rim of the circle straight above 90. Place the ruler across the center hole and touching your 90 mark. Draw a line from edge to edge of the circle, going across the center and touching 90. Label both ends of this line "90."

6. Position the protractor again as you did in step 5. Mark the places on the outer rim above 60° and also above 30°. Draw lines and label the points as you did in Step 5. When

you're finished, your dial should look like figure 3.

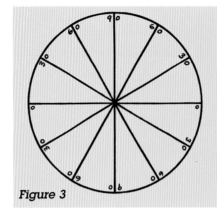

Figure 3

7. Paint the dial, and use a fine-point marker to number the angles.
8. To make the sighting arm, have an adult help you drill a hole in the middle of the wooden stick. Paint the sides and ends of the stick.
9. When the paint has dried completely, assemble the astrolabe. Put a washer on the bolt and slide the bolt into the hole in the wood. Slip another washer over the bolt, and then push the bolt through the hole in the center of the dial. Thread the wing nut onto the bolt end, and tighten it to keep the stick from moving around.
10. Use the scissors to cut the straw the same length as the stick.
11. Push the two pins through the straw about 1 inch (2.5 cm) in from each end, and then push the pins into the wooden stick.
12. Use the awl or nail to poke a small hole ¼ inch (6 mm) in from the edge of the cardboard at both of the 90° marks.
13. Loop a 10-inch (25.4 cm) piece of string through one of the holes. Slide the nuts onto the string and make a knot. Tie another 10-inch (25.4 cm) piece of string in a loop through the other hole.

To use the astrolabe, hang it by the loop from your outstretched arm, a tree branch, or a large nail in the side of a building so that the instrument hangs freely. To measure the altitude of a star, move the wooden sighting arm so that you can sight the star through the straw. Read the angle that the arm is pointing to. That's the altitude of the star—the number of degrees above the horizon. If you want to measure your own latitude, see page 19.

You could do the same thing with the sun, but unless you want to end up like the blind sailors who frequented the crews of many ships way back when, don't ever stare directly at the sun. To measure the altitude of the sun, hold the astrolabe by the loop so that the sun casts a shadow either above or below the sighting arm. Move the arm until the shadow of the stick disappears. (You'll still be able to see the shadow of the spacer washers.) The arm will be pointing directly at the sun, and you can read the dial to learn the altitude of the sun without looking at it.

14

Oh, Drat, the World Ain't Flat

It isn't easy finding where you are on a sphere that's floating around in space (especially one with more than 196,000,000 square miles [509,600,000 km²] of land and sea!). There aren't any edges or corners, and technically speaking, there isn't a top or bottom either. And since we do live on a round world, a system had to be devised to help folks pinpoint exactly where they were. Most sane people agree these days that the North Pole is the top and the South Pole is the bottom. There's even an imaginary line that acts as the edge of the Earth. It's called the Prime Meridian, and it runs from the North Pole through Greenwich, England to the South Pole. This same line on the other side of the world is called the International Date Line (see page 22). Another line, drawn around the middle of the world, is the equator. After that, there are four lines both north and south of the equator and a total of 24 lines up and down. All these lines dissect the world into a useful grid that chops up the world into imaginary pieces.

The lines above and below the equator are called "latitude lines," and they're used to determine one's distance either north (N) or south (S) of the equator. They're measured in degrees 70 miles (112 km) apart. The up and down lines are called "meridians" or "longitude lines," and they're used to determine one's distance east (E) or west (W) of the Prime Meridian. These lines are measured in terms of the 360 degrees of a circle and are essential for pinpointing location, which is especially helpful if you're traveling one of the world's oceans and have no landmarks to help you. ("Take a left at the big school of dolphins!") Each 15 degrees represents one hour of rotation of the Earth.

If you have trouble keeping latitude and longitude straight in your mind (as most people who don't have to navigate on a regular basis do), remember that LATitude rhymes with FLATitude, and that latitude lines run flat, north or south of the equator. If that's too punny for you, make up your own (just don't make fun of ours—it works).

LATITUDE & LONGITUDE AROUND THE WORLD • LATITUDE & LONGITU

The equator: 0° latitude   The North Pole: 90° N   The South Pole: 90°S

The Prime Meridian: 0° longitude   The International Date Line: 180° longitude

More on page 19

The Gulf of Guinea: 0°, 0°   The Pacific Ocean, near the Gilbert Islands: 0°, 180° (where the equator and International Dateline meet)   Paris, France: 48° 50' N, 2° 20' E*

* Each degree of latitude or longitude can be broken down into 60 minutes, which look like this: 44'. These minutes help you pinpoint location even more accurately when a location doesn't appear exactly on the latitude or longitude line.

CROSS STAFF

If an old-time mariner didn't use an astrolabe while attempting a lengthy sea journey, chances are he used a cross staff instead. The cross staff, also called a "sighting stick" or "Jacob's staff," is regarded as one of the oldest navigational instruments, and it was used as early as the 1300s to measure the altitude of stars, which allowed sailors to find their latitude, tell time, and find their direction at night.

WHAT YOU NEED
- Piece of wood, 1 x 2 x 17 inches (2.5 x 5.1 x 43.2 cm)
- Handsaw
- Sandpaper
- Piece of wood, ¼ x 1½ x 36 inches (.6 x 3.8 x 91.4 cm)
- Ruler
- Pencil
- Drill, with a bit slightly wider than the carriage bolts
- 2 carriage bolts, 2 inches (5.1 cm) long, with wing nuts
- Yardstick
- Protractor
- Acrylic craft paints
- Paintbrush
- Black, permanent marker

WHAT YOU DO
1. Saw the 17-inch-long (43.2 cm) piece of wood into two pieces—one 5 inches (12.7 cm) long and the other 12 inches (30.5 cm) long. Sand the ends of all the pieces of wood.

2. Use the ruler and the pencil to mark the center of the 5-inch (12.7 cm) piece of wood.

3. Lay the 36-inch (91.4 cm) piece of wood crossways over this center mark. Draw a line along each side of the long piece of wood. Remove the long piece of wood, and make two large dots. They should be centered and just outside each of the two lines you drew (see figure 1 on page 18).

4. Drill a hole through the 5-inch (12.7 cm) piece of wood at each of the two large dots.

5. Center the 12-inch (30.5 cm)

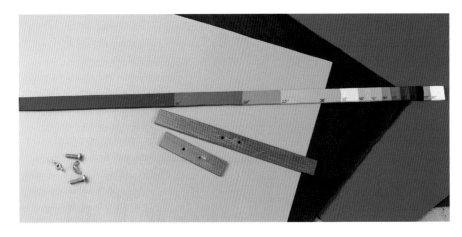

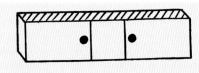

Figure 1

piece of wood under the 5-inch (12.7 cm) piece (figure 2). Stick the pencil down each drilled hole to

Figure 2

mark the wood underneath. Drill holes in the marked spots on this piece of wood, too.

6. Test the assembly by placing the 36-inch-long (91.4 cm) piece of wood between the holes in the two other pieces and slipping the bolts through the two pairs of holes. The wood should fit easily between the bolts. Tighten the wing nuts to hold the wood in position (figure 3).

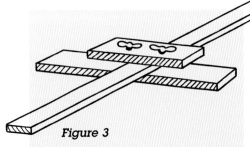

Figure 3

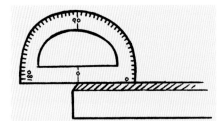

Figure 4

7. If everything fits, you can mark the angles on the staff. Lay the cross staff on the floor. Loosen the wing nuts, and slide the crosspiece—the two pieces of wood bolted together—down to about 4 inches (10.2 cm) from one end of the long stick. Place the protractor along the opposite end of the long stick (figure 4).

8. You'll notice that the protractor has angles marked going from 0 to 90 (straight up) to 180. Place the yardstick from the top of the crosspiece to the end of the long stick over the protractor. Slide the crosspiece (and push the yardstick so that it stays in contact with both crosspiece and long stick) so that the yardstick lies along the 10° line of the protractor (figure 5).

9. Draw a line across the flat surface of the long stick, using the side of the crosspiece that is closest to the

protractor as a guide. When the crosspiece is in this position, the reading will be 10°.

10. Now mark 15°, following the directions from steps 8 and 9. Continue marking every 5 degrees until you come to the end of the long stick. You should be able to get up to 65° or 70°.

11. Take the instrument completely apart to paint it. Paint one color between 0° and 10°, another color between 10° and 15°, and so on. After you have painted it, draw over the numbers with black marker so they can be easily read.

12. When the paint's completely dry, put the cross staff back together.

HOW TO USE YOUR CROSS STAFF

Go outside at night. Loosen the wing nuts a little so you can slide the crosspiece. Hold the long piece at eye level, with the higher numbers toward you. Sight a star along

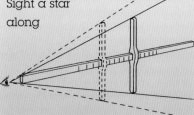

the edge of the staff and the top edge of the crosspiece. Slide the crosspiece until it lines up with your line of sight. Read the number closest to where the crosspiece crosses the long piece of wood. That is the altitude of the star. See page 19 to find your latitude.

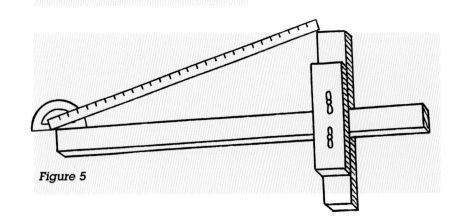

Figure 5

LOST? THANK YOUR LUCKY STARS

Many an old-time sea dweller thanked his or her lucky stars while traveling the open seas. Why? Because without the stars, they'd be lost. North of the equator, seafaring travelers relied on the North Star (a.k.a. Polaris) since it always appears in the same direction and can help locate one's latitude. The North Star is at the end of the handle of the Little Dipper. Now, that's great for sailors north of the equator, but what about folks south of the equator? They have their own stars to thank: the four stars of the Southern Cross constellation.

To find your latitude, measure the angle from the horizon to a pole star. (Use your astrolabe or cross staff.) Your latitude will be equal to the angle between the horizon and the pole star. If you're using the North Star as your pole star, your latitude is north of the equator, if you're using the Southern Cross as your pole star, your latitude is south of the equator.

For example, you're lost somewhere north of the equator and all you have is your trusty astrolabe or cross staff with you (good thing you packed it!). You discover that the North Star is 30° above the horizon at dusk. That means you're 30° above the equator, or 30° N.

30°

LATITUDE & LONGITUDE AROUND THE WORLD • LATITUDE & LONGITUDE

Tokyo, Japan: 35° 40' N, 139° 30' E

Sydney, Australia: 33° 53' S, 151° 10'E

Rio de Janeiro, Brazil: 22° 50' S, 43° W

Where your authors live: 35° 36' N, 82° 33' W (look it up!)

Where the *Titanic* sank: 41° N, 50° W

Your hometown: _____ N or S, _____ E or W

To find the exact opposite side of the world of your hometown, take your latitude, and change its direction. For example, the opposite of 22 °N is 22° S. For longitude, take your longitude—for this example, let's say it's 43° W—and subtract it from 180° (180-43=137). Then switch directions. The longitude of this place is 137° E. So the location opposite of 22° N, 43° W is 22° S, 137° E.

A TOTALLY USEFUL COMPASS

Nobody knows who invented the compass, though many cultures would like to take credit for it. The Chinese may have been using compasses for over 2,000 years. The Vikings used magnetized needles to guide them on their journeys. Whoever truly invented the compass, the truth remains that the compass was and still is an explorer's best friend.

Today's compass is a combination of the ancient compass rose, which had 32 points with the names of the winds, and a magnetized needle (a design that hasn't changed much in 800 years). That's all. Most make-it-yourself compasses are okay, but need water to make them work. This design is handy, compact, and pretty neat looking, if we do say so ourselves.

WHAT YOU NEED

- Two-piece plastic capsule with hang tab (available at craft stores)*
- White and black acrylic craft paint
- Paintbrush
- Ruler
- Permanent marker
- Metal sewing needle
- Thread
- Scissors
- $1/4$ x $1/4$-inch (6 x 6 mm) piece of cork
- Tape
- Refrigerator magnet
- Yarn or twine

*Make sure the two halves snap together tightly; if not, then you'll need to use glue or tape to keep them together.

WHAT YOU DO

1. Paint the outside of one of the capsule halves with white paint and let it dry. Next, paint over the white paint with black or another color of your choice. The inside of the capsule half should look white while the outside is black.

2. Use the ruler to make a cross over the open end of the capsule. Mark the letter for each direction at the ends of each line with the marker (figure 1).

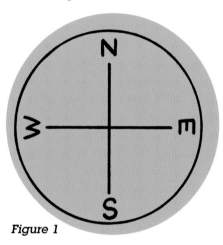

Figure 1

3. Thread the sewing needle with the thread and pass the needle through the center of the cork. Tie a knot in one end of the string so you can't pull it out of the cork (figure 2). Tape the other end of the string to the top of the unpainted half of the capsule.

4. Magnetize the sewing needle by rubbing the refrigerator magnet along it in one direction. Do not rub the magnet back and forth; rather, begin at the point close to you and sweep the magnet down the needle away from you several times.

5. Insert the sewing needle through the center of the cork so it's balanced when you let it hang freely.

6. Put the capsule halves together so the needle hangs freely. Make sure the needle doesn't touch the capsule walls (shorten the string or use a smaller needle if it does).

7. Rotate the capsule so the needle points to N. Find a commercial compass and compare. If they don't match within a few degrees, you may want to try to re-magnetize your needle.

8. Cut a piece of yarn, twine, or cord to make a strap for the compass to hang from. Pass the twine through the hang tab on the capsule, and tie the loose ends in a knot. Now go explore!

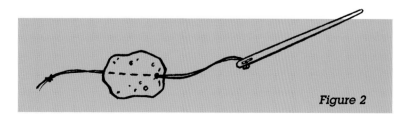

Figure 2

Happy Birthday

to You x 2

The few, lucky survivors of Magellan's voyage around the world (even Magellan didn't make it) realized something peculiar. They had kept very good records of the number of days they'd been away, and when they returned home, they realized they had lost a day! Where did it go? They lost their day when they crossed the International Date Line, an imaginary line that's on the opposite side of the Prime Meridian. If you're standing on one side of the IDL and your friend is standing on the other side, you'd be enjoying different days of the week. Technically, you could celebrate your birthday twice: stand just east of the line on your birthday, and then the next day, jump over the line and celebrate again. Don't hold your breath, though, waiting for more presents.

THE GREAT AGE OF DISCOVERY IN PERSPECTIVE

During the great age of exploration and discovery that helped end the dreadful Middle Ages, whole new worlds were discovered (though the people already living in these new worlds had, of course, already discovered them!). And each new discovery changed the world of the explorers and of the people already on the lands "discovered." It would be almost impossible to grasp today what it must have felt like to live during this time. So, try this: Imagine a space mission returning with news that they've found life on another planet, and they've brought some of these folks to Earth for a visit. What would your first reaction be? Surprise, shock, disbelief, fear, relief? What would you want to know about them? What could you learn from them? What could they learn from you? What do they have that could be of benefit to society? Can they play soccer? These are some questions that came to mind (okay, perhaps they didn't care much about soccer) as new worlds and people discovered each other on Earth. History, however, has shown that greed often got the best of many explorers, some of whom quickly became conquerors. Do you think we would seek to conquer new worlds in space today? Or do you think we've grown as a world society so that we'd instead seek to be peaceful neighbors who can learn and benefit from each other?

Soccer? Where I come from we call it football.

Amaze Your Friends
Prove the World Isn't Flat!

Okay, perhaps your friends will not be amazed, though it certainly is interesting that astronomers 2,000 years before Columbus's journeys not only knew Earth was spherical, but had accurately figured out its diameter. Anyway, if you have a friend who doubts the world is round, you can share this quick and easy activity to help him out. (He needs it!)

WHAT YOU NEED
- An ocean, with a ship sailing away toward the horizon
- A friend, preferably one who has lived in a cave much of his life
- A lunar eclipse (optional)

WHAT YOU DO

1. Bring your friend to the ocean and stand along the shoreline. Look for ships sailing out to sea. Watch the ship as it gets smaller and smaller. If the world was flat, you and your friend would see the whole ship get smaller and smaller until it was too far away to see. However, watch what happens. As the ship moves toward the horizon, the ship's hull disappears first—as if the ship were slowly slipping off the edge of the world!

2. If that doesn't convince your friend, find out when the next lunar eclipse is and make sure your friend checks out the shadow Earth casts on the moon. It's round!

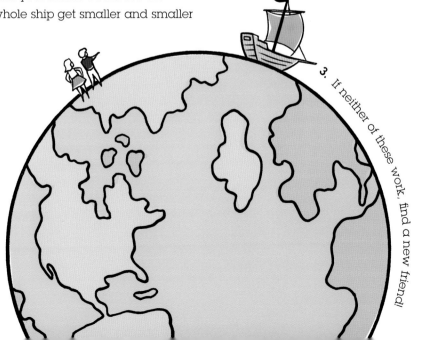

3. If neither of these work, find a new friend!

STILL LOST?
Try a GPS Receiver

LOOK UP. SMILE. Gotcha! There are thousands of satellites up there in space taking pictures, recording information, and sending signals. But there are 24 super-cool satellites (called the Global Positioning System or GPS) orbiting 11,000 miles (17,600 km) above us that can help you figure out exactly where you're located. The GPS was developed for military purposes by the United States, but they now kindly let anyone use it. And for about the cost of three or four copies of this book, you could own a GPS receiver. It's a small, hand-held device that looks a little bit like a calculator, and it picks up signals from at least four of the 24 GPS satellites. These satellites send longitude, latitude, and altitude to the receiver. Most receivers then use a world map that's stored in its memory to pinpoint your location. It can be used anywhere on Earth: in a car, on a plane, on a boat, while hiking, or just standing around (as long as you're outside). Some receivers can also trace your path across a map as you travel and determine how fast you're going. A GPS receiver can be placed in a car and act as a speedometer and odometer. Some models will also figure out when you'll get where you're going.

HOUSE SUNDIAL CLOCK

Another ancient instrument that was important for early geographers was the sundial clock. These not only helped keep time, but could also figure out location, when the seasons changed, and the length of a day. A sundial was also instrumental in figuring out the circumference of the Earth 2,000 years before Columbus bumped into the Americas. You can turn your whole house into a sundial clock by observing the sun's movement around it throughout the day.

WHAT YOU NEED

- 10 x 10-inch (25.4 x 25.4 cm) piece of cardboard
- Pencil
- Old magazines
- Scissors
- Glue
- Compass
- Acrylic craft paint
- Paintbrush
- Journal or paper
- Tall, thin objects, such as rulers or vases
- 6-inch (15.2 cm) cardboard circle
- Foam brush
- Awl or nail
- 1/4-inch (6 mm) quartz, battery-operated clock movement with hands*

*available at craft stores

WHAT YOU DO

1. On the cardboard square, draw a floor plan of all the rooms on the main floor of your home.

2. Cut out magazine images to match the rooms, and glue them in the appropriate place on the floor plan.

3. Stand in the center of the main floor of the house with a compass, and locate each of the four directions.

Figure 1

Write N for north on the cardboard square in the northernmost room in your house, E for east in the room that faces east, and so on. Use paint or markers to make the letters stand out.

4. One morning, wake up at sunrise (come on, you can do it!) and write down the time as the sun moves through each room in the house. To help figure out when the sun is directly in line with a particular side of the house, place a tall, thin object on every windowsill and record the time when the object's shadow falls straight behind it (figure 1).

5. Decorate the cardboard circle to look like a clockface, and write the numbers 1 through 12 around the dial, with 6 at the top of the clock (see photo). We painted half of our dial yellow to represent daylight and midnight blue for night. Use another clockface as a guide for spacing the numbers, or follow the pattern on page 140.

6. Poke a hole through the centers of the cardboard square and circle, then slide the shaft of the clockworks through the hole in each. The dial should fit on top of the square and spin easily.

7. Spin the dial so that the hour for sunrise matches up with the room the sun first hits in the morning. Throughout the day, as the sun moves around your home, you should notice that the hour on the clock matches the room with the most sunlight. If this doesn't happen, try adjusting the size of your clockface and the distance between the numbers. **Note:** You'll have to adjust the number dial after a few days, since the sun rises at different times over the course of the year.

THIS AIN'T NO SUNDIAL!

Back in the time before wristwatches and other semi-accurate timepieces existed, if you asked someone what time it was, he or she might say, "My stomach's rumblin' so it must be suppertime." Today, relying on your stomach noises or even a digital watch you found in a cereal box could make you late for school or make you miss your favorite TV show. (You shouldn't be watching TV anyway.) Ever wonder how we know *exactly* what time it is? Well, there are atomic clocks that keep super-accurate time. So good, in fact, that the most accurate one, the NIST-F1 in Boulder, Colorado, won't lose or gain a second for around 20 million years. How does it work? Basically, instead of using a pendulum (like a grandfather clock), atomic clocks use (you guessed it) atoms to determine the duration of one second. These clocks are used to operate the Global Positioning System (see page 23), to help navigate spacecraft, and to synchronize telecommunication and computer operations. And although you can't fit one on your wrist, you can buy a clock that automatically synchronizes itself to an atomic clock.

The NIST F-1; courtesy of the National Institute of Standards and Technology; photo by Geoffrey Wheeler

STILL, STILL LOST?
FIND LONGITUDE & WIN BIG BUCKS!

It was one thing for early maritime explorers to be able to find their latitude, but without knowing their longitude it was still pretty dangerous to venture overseas. The problem? Even though longitude could be figured out on land, you needed an extremely accurate clock, and no such thing existed before the 18th century that could withstand the rough treatment of a sea voyage. It became such a huge problem that kings and governments offered big cash rewards for the first person who

could create an accurate timekeeper on a ship. (England's parliament offered 20,000 pounds, which is equivalent to about $1 million today!) Enter our hero, John Harrison (1693-1776), an uneducated (which bothered the snooty scientists back then) carpenter from Yorkshire, England.

Whoa, back up? A clock to help find location? Yup, that's right. Remember, longitude lines are the ones that go up and down from both poles. The Earth takes 24 hours to complete one 360° spin. If you divide 360 by 24 you get

This marine chronomether was made in Paris, France in 1776. Courtesy of the Clock and Watch Museum Beyer Zurich.

15. That's the number of degrees the Earth spins in one hour ($1/24$ of the Earth's full spin). So, if you know what time it is in one location, let's say Greenwich, England, home of the Prime Meridian, and you know what time it is where you are right now, you can figure out your longitude east or west of the Prime Meridian. Here's an example: If it's 4 p.m. in Greenwich and 12 p.m. where your ship is located, you're four time zones west of the Prime Meridian. That's 60° west longitude (15 x 4 = 60) or 60° W. Or say it's 9 a.m. in Greenwich and 12 p.m. where you're located. That's three time zones or 45° E.

Though it took Harrison much of his adult life to create this precise clock (called a *chronometer*), it was a great success, though the best scientific minds of Europe had to have their arms twisted by King George before they coughed up the big bucks that Harrison so rightfully deserved.

Watch the news some time and see if the newsroom has a bunch of clocks with different times on them. They're showing the times in several different cities around the world. If you check out a map of the world's time zones, you'll notice that the time stays the same as you move along longitude lines, but changes as you move across latitudes. Create your own time-zone clock so you can keep track of what time it is in other countries where friends or family live.

TIME-ZONE CLOCK

WHAT YOU NEED

- Atlas
- Wooden board, $^3/_4$ x $5^1/_2$ x 24 inches (1.9 x 14 x 61 cm)
- Ruler
- Pencil
- Drill, with a bit slightly wider than the shaft of the clockworks
- 4 sets of $^3/_4$-inch (1.9 cm) quartz, battery-operated clock movements with hands*
- Acrylic craft paint
- Paintbrush
- $5^1/_2$-inch-diameter (14 cm) circle (a bowl or lid) for making the clock faces, or a compass (not the one for finding your direction)
- World times

*available at craft stores

WHAT YOU DO

1. Choose four places around the world that interest you and compare their times. Look for symbols in the atlas that represent those countries, cities, etc., to use as designs for your clock faces.

2. Using the ruler, find the center of the board, and draw a straight line across the center of the board from one end to the other.

3. Starting at one end of the wooden board, mark an X in the center of the board at 3, 9, 15, and 21 inches (7.6, 22.9, 38.1, and 53.3 cm).

4. Drill a hole through the X at each spot, and then check to make sure that the clockwork shafts fit in them. If your holes are too small, use a larger drill bit.

5. Paint the entire board with a color you like as a background for the clocks. Let it dry.

6. Make a $5^1/_2$-inch-diameter (14 cm) circle around each of the drilled holes, using the bowl or lid as a pattern. If you have a compass, use that instead.

7. Paint the clock faces with symbols of the locations you chose. Here, we replicated the flags of China, Kenya, Argentina, and Australia.

8. Refer to a clock face, or use the figure on page 140 for spacing your numbers around each dial to match the speed of the clock.

9. Assemble the clockworks according to the manufacturer's directions. Set each clock to the current time for the locations you chose. You can use the atlas to help you figure out the times compared to local time, or you could search the Internet for "world times" to find accurate times for almost any location.

DREAM TRAVEL BOX

Though the world is now a familiar place for geographers, that doesn't mean the world is familiar to you! Imagine you could go anywhere in the world. Would you want to be some-place warm, or do you love snow? Do you dream of the ocean or trekking up in the mountains? What if you could go to a place where you could watch volcanoes erupt?

Whatever your dream place is, you can find information about it by searching on the Internet, looking for books at the library, and picking up brochures from travel agents. With a little planning, you could make it there one day. Until then, you can dream and collect all the things you find about this place in a special box to look through from time to time until your dream becomes reality.

WHAT YOU NEED

- Shoebox with lid
- Acrylic craft paint
- Paintbrush
- Images from magazines, books, brochures, or from the Internet that relate to your dream place
- Scissors or craft knife
- Small map of your dream location
- Craft glue
- Foam brush
- Decoupage glue

WHAT YOU DO

1. Paint the entire box a color you like.

2. With scissors, cut out the images you want on the box from the materials you've gathered. Place each image on the piece of cardboard and carefully cut along their outlines.

3. Glue the small map of the country you're hoping to travel to on the lid of the box.

4. Cut images to fit inside of the map, trimming the outside images to fit the contours of the border.

5. When you've filled in the map, outline it with a bright color of paint so it'll stand out. Decorate the rest of the box as you want.

7. Use the foam brush to cover each side of the box and lid with a thin layer of decoupage glue to seal and protect your collage.

8. Fill your box with information that can help you get to your dream location someday. Use your box and its contents to convince your parents that they may like to go there as well (and take you, of course)!

Before the World Was a Spherical Planet Orbiting the Sun...

A MYTH IS A STORY WITH A PURPOSE, and each ancient culture had its own set of stories that tried to explain why the world is the way it is. Stories were created to tell of how the world began, why storms happened, or why we die. Before science provided answers to some of the world's mysteries, people told stories to help explore these mysteries. These stories took the form of rituals, artworks, dances, or simple stories told to children before they went to bed. They helped the world seem more understandable, less scary, as well as more beautiful. And although they may seem farfetched, the message behind myths had an important meaning for those who told, listened, and believed them.

Some of the most fascinating myths include how ancient cultures thought the world began and what it looked like. The Vikings believed there were nine worlds, including Earth, all of which were arranged in three layers around Yggdrasil, a huge ash tree at the center of the universe. The ancient Egyptians thought the sky was a tent that stretched between mountains at the four corners of the Earth. The ancient Greeks believed Earth was a flat disk surrounded by a world ocean. In the Hindu Vedas tradition, a tree of knowledge held up the universe. Here's one particularly beautiful myth from the Iroquois of the northeast United States:

Before Earth as we know it was formed, all that existed was water, where many animals lived, and sky, where a chief and his people lived. One day the chief's young, pregnant wife went searching for some herbs for her husband. As she dug near the Great Tree, which bore fruits and flowers of all kinds, a hole opened up. Curious, she leaned forward, grabbing the tree for support, but she lost her balance and tumbled into the hole, holding only a handful of seeds.

The birds that flew over the water saw her falling and flew up and eased her fall with their outspread wings. Muskrat then quickly dove beneath the water and brought up handfuls of soft mud, which he placed on the back of a snapping turtle. The woman landed on the turtle's back, the mud became the earth, and trees and grass grew from the seeds in the woman's hand. To this day, the world rests on the back of the giant turtle, and when he moves, there are earthquakes and floods.

MARCO POLO TRAVEL JOURNAL

Marco Polo (1254–1324) didn't have a travel agent, nor did he have transportation. That didn't stop him, however, from traveling thousands of miles into the heart of Asia. Not bad for a guy who got around 600 years before anyone ever heard of airplanes and cars. However, Marco Polo did something else remarkable: He wrote down what he saw, heard, ate, learned, and experienced, and his writings continue to affect history today.

Now, once you've decided on a place to visit and figured out how to get there, you may want to keep a journal of your own. A journal will help you remember and enjoy your travels long after they're over. It can be part notebook, part sketchbook, and even part scrapbook, in which you record in words, pictures, and small souvenirs the events, places, and surprises you encountered. Marco would be proud.

WHAT YOU NEED
- Journal or sketchbook of your choice
- Pictures of old maps
- Scissors
- Craft glue
- Gold foil and adhesive
- Foam brush
- Ribbon
- Decoupage glue

WHAT YOU DO

1. Decide what you want to decorate your journal cover with, then cut the image(s) to size and arrange it/them on the cover.

2. Evenly spread glue on the back of the image you're using and carefully smooth it in place on the journal cover.

3. Cut three strips of gold foil, each long enough to fit along an edge of the journal that you want to cover. Spread the gold foil adhesive with a brush along the cover where you want the gold to stick, then wait a few minutes until it turns clear.

4. Place each strip of gold foil evenly along the edge of the journal. Use the handle end of the foam brush to rub back and forth on the foil to make it stick to the cover.

5. Carefully peel back the foil. Repeat steps 3 and 4 for a thicker layer of gold foil.

6. Measure the ribbon against the design on your cover and cut it to fit where you want it.

7. Spread a thin line of glue under the ribbon and press it in place.

8. With the foam brush, spread a thin coat of decoupage glue over the entire cover to seal and protect it. Fill your travel journal with sketches, photographs, poems, thoughts, and memories of places you visit, be they weekend trips with your family or long summer adventures.

"HEY, WHAT ABOUT ME?!"

Marco Polo's a pretty impressive guy, but we could have also called this journal the Chang Ch'ien Travel Journal. Sure "Chang Ch'ien" may not not be a household name, but when it comes to explorers, Chang Ch'ien is one of the greatest! *Huh?* That's right! Chang Ch'ien covered a lot of the same ground Polo did, but from the other direction! He left the capital of China in 138 B.C.E. as an ambassador, hoping to sign a treaty with a tribe 2,000 miles (3,200 km) away. After 13 years (many spent as a prisoner), he returned to China, not with the treaty, but with a ton of information on the history, geography, and culture of Central Asia, Persia, Arabia, and even the Roman Empire. Chang Ch'ien's travels led to increased trade and the most famous overland trade route ever: the Silk Road. So go ahead, give the guy a break and call your journal the Chang Ch'ien Travel Journal. He'd appreciate it.

WORLDLY PLACE MATS

When Christopher Columbus returned from the Americas, he needed to bring evidence that he had actually been somewhere. Though he didn't find gold or valuable spices, he did return with something that became quite a hit in Europe: sweet potatoes.

After you return from your traveling adventures and empty your pockets and bags, turn your valuable "evidence" into these lasting tributes to your dream vacation. You can even serve sweet potatoes on them.

WHAT YOU NEED
- Poster board
- Scissors
- Stencil letters (optional)
- Marker (optional)
- Craft knife (optional)
- Mementos from your trip
- Glue
- Clear adhesive shelf paper

WHAT YOU DO
1. Cut pieces of poster board to the size of your proposed place mats.
2. If you want, use the stencil letters to write the name of the country you visited on top of the place mat, and use the craft knife to cut out the letters.
3. Design your place mat by arranging your mementos on one of the pieces of poster board until you're happy with how it looks.
4. Remove the mementos, and one by one, glue them to the poster board.
5. Cut a piece of the shelf paper slightly larger than the place mat. Peel off the backing and place the shelf paper sticky side up onto your work surface.
6. Carefully lay your place mat on the shelf paper and smooth it down.
7. Cut a second piece of shelf paper and place it on top of the place mat.
8. Cut around the edges of the place mat until the shelf paper is the same length around the mat. Repeat until you have the number of place mats you want.

Chapter 2

Maps, Maps, & Even More Maps

A MAP IS A PICTURE OF A PLACE. Sounds simple. However, if the map below looks a little strange to you, then maps aren't as simple as you may think. You see, there is absolutely nothing wrong with this map. It shows the continents accurately, and all the place names are correct. What? It's upside down?! Says you. There's no upside down in space. Plus, Earth is spherical, and sphere's don't generally have tops and bottoms. This map is just as accurate as any map you're used to seeing. So there! Knowing where you are is a fundamental concept of geography, and maps are pretty good tools for the job. However, as you can see, maps can be funny things. Sure, they're good at presenting information you need about a place, but since mapmakers have to make decisions about what to show and how to show them, maps also become good at *telling* us how to think about places. They also tell us about what people in the past knew and didn't know about the world, or what was important to them. Maps say a lot about who we are and hold clues about not only the mapmakers but the people who use the maps. This chapter explores maps (as you've probably already figured out): how to make them, how to use them, how to understand them, as well as how to have some fun with them.

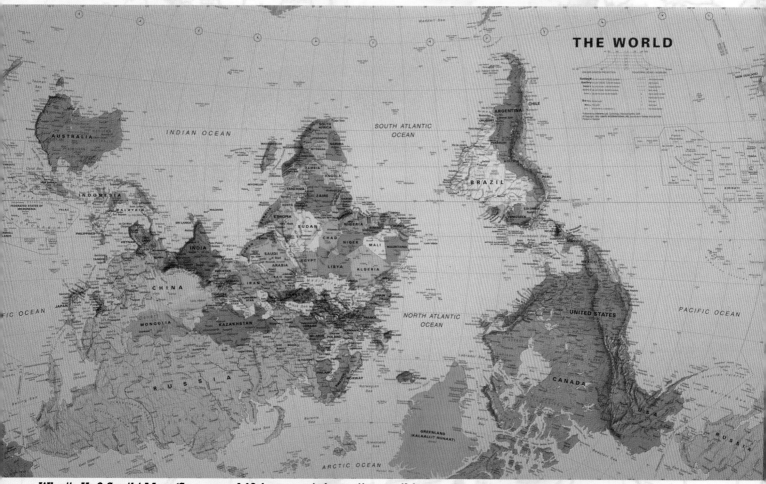

What's Up? South! Map (See page 143 for more information on this map.)

BECOME A CARTOGRAPHER IN ONE DAY
(Plus or Minus Several Years of Study and Practice)

It's a plain, old fact that some people would rather have a beautiful map that isn't all that accurate than a map that strictly gives good information about a location. A cartographer is another word for a mapmaker, and it's a cartographer's job to combine science and art to create the world's maps. This project delves into the science of making a map. For the art of making a map, see page 37. Now, most mapmakers would get upset at us if we said you could become a great cartographer simply by reading this book. So, we won't say that. (Angry mapmakers make us nervous.) However, we have no problem telling you how to make a simple map using only a compass, a tape measure, and a protractor. This map will be accurate and it's fun. If you run into any angry mapmakers, don't tell them where we live.

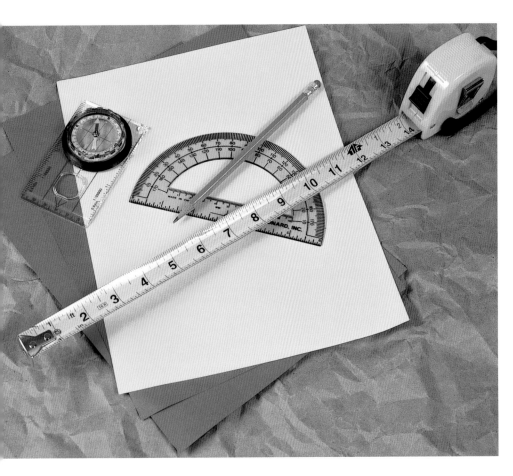

WHAT YOU NEED
- Tape measure
- Paper
- Clipboard
- Calculator (optional)
- Rock
- Pencil
- Compass, with degrees noted on the face
- Ruler
- Protractor

WHAT YOU DO
1. Find a good place to map. Pick a place that has some fun features, such as a park, playground, or backyard.
2. Find the scale of your map. To do this, first measure the perimeter of the area you wish to map. Then divide the size of the area by the size of your paper. Here are two examples, one for the ever-dwindling feet and inches crowd, and

N

X

1 inch = 12 feet   1 cm = 2 m

another for the vast metric crowd:
A. Say you want to map a playground that's 120 x 120 feet, and your paper is 10 x 10 inches. First, convert feet into inches by multiplying 120 by 12, which equals 1,440 inches. Then divide 1,440 inches by 10, which is 144 inches. The scale is

1:144. This means that 1 inch on the map equals 144 inches or 12 feet.
B. Say you want to map a playground that's 40 x 40 meters, and your paper is 20 x 20 centimeters. First, convert meters into centimeters by multiplying 40 by 100, which equals 4,000. Then divide 4,000

centimeters by 20, which equals 200 centimeters. The scale is 1:200. This means that 1 centimeter on the map equals 200 centimeters or 2 meters.
3. Locate the middle of the area you've chosen to map and mark it with the rock. This is the point where you will make your measurements.

Mark this spot on your paper. Use the clipboard to make drawing while standing easier.

4. Stand over the rock, and find north with the compass. Draw a line from the center point to show north. Use a ruler to get a straight line (figure 1).

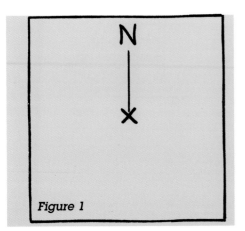
Figure 1

5. In order to figure out where to plot your objects on your map, you'll need to measure angles and distances. To measure an angle, you'll use the compass to measure how many degrees from north each object is. For example, say you're mapping out a playground, and the first item you want to plot is a slide. While you're standing at the center point, face the slide and hold the compass directly in front of you at eye level (figure 2). Notice where north is and then write down how

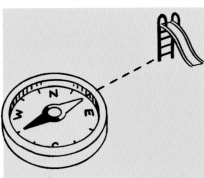
Figure 2

many degrees the slide is from north (say 60°).

6. Place the protractor over the center point on your map and mark the angle of your bearing with a pencil line. This is the direction of the slide (figure 3).

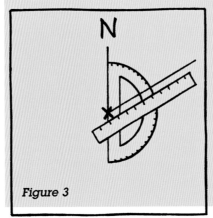
Figure 3

7. Measure how far away the object is from the center point (its distance) with the tape measure (let's say the slide was 10 meters] away).

8. Mark the distance, keeping in mind the scale you developed in step 2 —10 meters = 5 cm (figure 4).

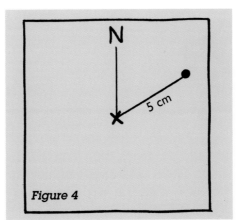
Figure 4

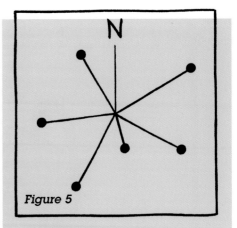
Figure 5

9. Follow steps 3 through 8 for every object you wish to include on your map (figure 5). When taking bearings on buildings or other large structures, take more than one bearing (use the buildings' corners). Since protractors have only 180 degrees, when you get a compass bearing that's more than 180° you'll have to do some subtracting. For example, say you take a bearing on a tree and it's 320° from north. Subtract 180 from 320 and you get 140. Place your protractor so that 180 is at the top of the map (pointing north) and read off 140°. This will end up being your 320° bearing.

10. After you've mapped all the objects in your area, you can draw in the objects and then erase your lines. Don't forget to show your scale on the map somewhere.

ANTIQUE MAP & CASE

This project focuses more on the art of mapmaking—in other words, making them pretty and cool. Most maps created during the Age of Exploration were stunning to look at, even if you couldn't find where in the world you were on it. If you're fascinated with these old maps, here's your chance to make one for yourself. You can use it to lead to the time capsule on page 73, or simply to decorate your room.

page 73

WHAT YOU NEED

- Drawing paper
- Pens, markers, crayons, and/or colored pencils
- Ruler
- Black tea bag soaked in hot water
- Use of an oven
- Candle or lighter
- Mailing tube
- Scissors
- Fabric strips
- Paper
- Ribbon
- Craft glue

WHAT YOU DO

1. Draw your map on the drawing paper with markers, colored pencils, crayons, and/or pens. (See page 34 for information on creating maps.) Look at old maps for ideas for adding details, such as a compass rose in an antique-looking style.

2. When the ink on your map is dry, crumple the paper into a tight ball. Do this a few times until you think the map is sufficiently wrinkled.

3. Squeeze the excess water out of the tea bag, then blot the map with it. Wipe the tea bag all over the

paper, and firmly press the bag onto the paper in some spots to get darker stains.

4. Place the paper in the oven on the rack at 200°F (93°C) for a few

minutes until the paper is dry. Check the map often, as it'll dry quickly.

5. Ask a parent for help to use the lighter or candle to burn the edges of the paper to finish the antique look.

6. No treasure map is complete without its case. Cut a mailing tube so the rolled-up map fits into it. Save the caps for both ends of the original tube to close the case.

7. Glue fabric scraps, paper, ribbon, and other exotic-looking materials onto the tube to make the case look fit for a king or queen's map.

OLD MAP PILLOWCASE OR ADVENTURE BACKPACK

Some old maps are so awesome looking you may want to make your own exotic map patches to personalize your everyday belongings. With the help of a computer and color printer, you can download and print historical maps and imagery straight from the Internet. Since most of these maps are in the public domain (meaning the original creator long ago passed away or the images were produced by and for a government agency), you can use them for your projects.

WHAT YOU NEED

- Computer with Internet access
- Photo-editing software (optional)
- Ink-jet color printer
- Iron-on transfer paper (available at office supply stores)
- Lightly colored backpack, pillow-case, or other cloth item to decorate
- Iron
- Colored pens or fabric paint (optional)

WHAT YOU DO

1. Check out sources for old maps and public-domain images, or do your own subject search on the Internet for sites with images you can download and print. If you have photo-editing software, you can work with the digital images you find to change their size to fit the object you want to decorate. If you don't have this software, then look for images you can print directly. You should print the images you like on plain paper to judge the quality and actual layout of the images before using the transfer paper. If you have a scanner, you could also scan pictures you like and print them out.

2. When you've experimented with the image you want and have a good printed version, load the transfer paper into the printer and print the image again.

3. Cut the excess transfer paper from around the image and center it on your backpack or pillowcase to make sure it'll fit well.

4. Follow the directions provided by the manufacturer of the transfer paper for ironing your image onto the fabric. Some helpful tips include:

- Smooth out any wrinkles in the fabric you're going to transfer the image onto, and work on a firm, flat surface.
- Be especially careful to press the iron down firmly for several seconds on the image, especially along the edges. Then run the iron over the entire surface for a few minutes to make sure the image has taken to the fabric.
- Let the transfer paper cool completely before trying to peel it off the object you're transferring to.
- Slowly and steadily peel the paper off the fabric. If you notice that the image has not completely transferred, stop pulling it up and smooth the paper back down and iron again.
- Make sure you're transferring onto light-colored fabrics, since images don't transfer well onto dark material.

5. You can highlight details of your image with permanent ink pens or fabric paint, or use paints and markers to add color to a black-and-white image.

GRID ART

WHAT YOU NEED

- Cool image you wish you could draw
- Tracing paper or graph paper
- Ruler
- Pencil
- Use of a photocopy machine

WHAT YOU DO

1. Cut a piece of tracing paper or graph paper to the size of the cool drawing you wish you could draw.

2. Draw straight, horizontal lines every 1 inch (2.5 cm) from one side of the page to the other. Use the ruler to make sure the lines are straight and spaced equally apart. Repeat with vertical lines every 1 inch (2.5 cm).

3. Decide whether you want your drawing to be bigger or smaller than the cool drawing, and enlarge or reduce the size of the grid you've drawn on the tracing paper with the photocopier. For example, if you want your image to be 20 percent larger, enlarge the size of the photocopied grid to 120 percent. Play with the "lighter/darker" buttons until your photocopied grid is very light.

4. Place the tracing paper over the cool drawing, and simply draw what you see in each square onto the same square on the photocopied paper. Voilà, you're an artist! We knew you had it in you. And that's how grids work on a map. Each square is simply a much smaller picture of the actual area it's showing.

Most maps that show locations in cities and towns have grids, which are horizontal and vertical lines that intersect to create boxes. These are not the same as latitude and longitude lines. This network of lines helps you find specific locations on the map. Usually columns are given numbers and rows are given letters, or vice versa. So if a road is located at B3, you can find the exact box in which that road is located. Here's a grid activity that not only shows you how grids work, but also how you can begin your career as an artist.

NEIGHBORHOOD MAP

As cool as maps are, they can't do and show everything. In fact, mapmakers are pretty particular about what they include in their maps. They can't possibly include everything there is to see—maps would be way too hard to read and decipher. So maps are drawn to show only what mapmakers and others consider very important.

That's one reason why your home most likely isn't highlighted on a map of your city. Sure your home's important to you, but it's not too important to the rest of the city. But sometimes maps omit too much, leaving you with a map that doesn't have enough information. You can fix that by personalizing a street map of your neighborhood to REALLY show what's there. You'll identify natural and cultural landmarks in your neighborhood not found on street maps, and talk with your neighbors and share your suggestions for the best routes for walking the dog, riding your bike, jogging, or skateboarding.

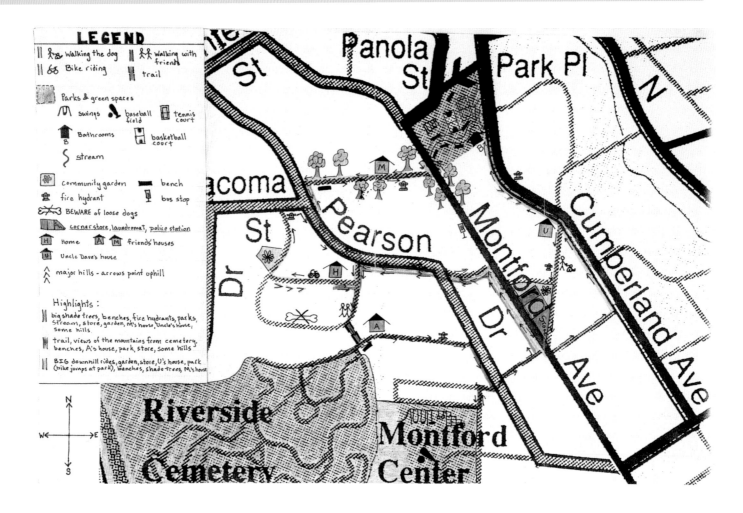

WHAT YOU NEED

- Notebook with a hard back or paper attached to a clipboard
- Street map that includes your neighborhood
- Use of a photocopy machine
- Ruler
- Colored pencils, crayons, or markers
- Pencil
- Eraser
- Black marker
- White correction fluid
- Glue
- Foam brush
- Compass

WHAT YOU DO

1. Let your dog take you for a walk (with guidance from you to stay on sidewalks and out of backyards). Let your dog lead the way around the neighborhood, and let your furry friend pick the next direction at intersections. Keep track of your route by writing it down in a notebook as you move from place to place. Write down the features your dog is attracted to, such as trees and fire hydrants, as well as the places you should avoid in the future. If you don't have a dog, keep reading.

2. Strap on a pair of inline skates, or hop on your bike, and highlight the best route through your neighborhood on the map. Highlight the best route for exploring with a friend. How are these routes different from the dog-walking route? Are any sections the same? How does landscape affect where and how roads are made and the shape of your neighborhood? What neighborhood improvements would you recommend to make the routes

even better and safer for walkers, dogs, or bike riders?

3. Use the zoom settings on a photocopier to enlarge the section of the street map that shows your neighborhood. Enlarge it until you can easily draw in details such as houses, trees, and signs. Your map will probably be large enough to work with when 3 inches equals 1 mile (7.6 cm equals 1.6 km). To figure this out, look at the original map and use the map scale to measure and locate a street that is 1 mile (1.6 km) long. Go to the enlarged map and measure the same street with a ruler. Keep enlarging this map until the street you're measuring becomes 3 inches (7.6 cm) long.

4. Refer to your notes and highlight your dog's path with a brightly colored marker, colored pencil, or crayon. Draw your house and other features that are important to your dog or to you.

5. In one corner of your map make a legend to explain all of the symbols you created for it. Cut a piece of blank paper and paste it over the part of your map where you want the legend to be. Decorate with the symbols you made and their meanings.

6. Fold your neighborhood map accordion-style into even sections for easy carrying.

7. Cut a photocopy of the original map to fit on the front of your map when it's folded up. Use the foam brush to spread the glue on the back of the photocopy and paste it to the front of your map.

8. Make a circle around your neighborhood. Decorate as you like.

9. Present your map to neighbors and share your suggestions for neighborhood improvements. If your neighborhood has an organized council or a representative who works with your town's government, send a map to them with your suggestions, and maybe your effort will make the improvements happen.

FAMILY MAPS

WHAT YOU NEED
- Your family
- Paper
- Markers

WHAT YOU DO

1. Have each family member map the same area, with your home as the center. Give them the streets they should map, and ask each of them to mark locations and landmarks. While they're doing the activity, you can do one yourself.

2. After everyone's done, compare the maps. What landmarks did a sibling choose that your dad or mom didn't choose? Why do you think that happened? Well, the same thing happens to real mapmakers. They may map the same area, but highlight different landmarks, due to their knowledge of the area or their reason for making the map.

"Hey, Dad, this is Heather. I'm in front of the candy shop. Can you pick me up? It's raining."

"No problem, tell me how to get to the candy shop."

"Take a left onto 9th Street, and then turn right when you see the bicycle shop."

"The what?"

"You know, the bicycle shop on 9th."

"Oh, you mean the shop next to the bank. Okay, I'll be right there."

Have you ever had to give directions to one of your parents and had trouble because they didn't know the landmarks you were using to direct them? Doesn't it seem odd to you that you can live in the same place as the rest of your family, and yet notice completely different landmarks? Try this map experiment with your family and see how the same thing could happen to cartographers.

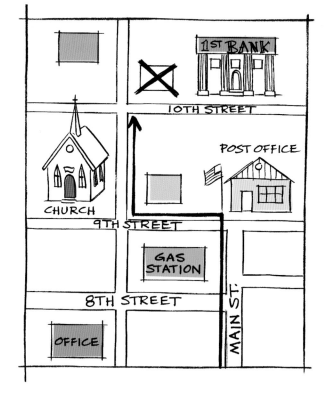

GLOBE YOUR FRIENDS

As you taught your friend in Chapter 1, the world is round (okay, technically it's a sphere). So, the only truly accurate map of Earth is a globe. (The best way to map a round object is with a round map.) Now, globes are great for classrooms and bedrooms, but they can get pretty hard to handle during a car trip or while out exploring. That's why we need flat maps, which are called "projections." These are great because you can fold them up and put them in your pocket. The only problem with flat maps is that when those nice cartographers take the time to project the curved earth onto a flat piece of paper, funny things start happening. Countries and oceans get stretched out and distorted. In fact, no matter how hard you try, a flat map will not be as accurate as a globe. Draw a map of the world on a grapefruit, and then carefully peel it. Go ahead, try it out. We'll wait....

...Now, try placing the rind onto a table. Not so easy, is it? First of all, there are gaps at the top and bottom. If you stretch the top and bottom so that they come together, the world at those places becomes distorted, and they appear much bigger than they actually are. In fact, if you stretch the globe out on a flat surface, almost all directions and distances between things are out of their proper places.

In this activity, you'll start with a flat photograph and cut away pieces until you can create a globe. Those extra pieces you end up cutting away represent all the extra pieces that have to be added to a flat map to make it look good! See page 49 for more on flat maps.

WHAT YOU NEED

- Template on page 141
- Use of a photocopy machine
- Pencil
- Your class picture or other image enlarged to 11 x 14 inches (27.9 x 35.6 cm)
- Cereal box
- 1 piece of colored paper, 11 x 14 inches (27.9 x 35.6 cm)
- Scissors or craft knife
- Craft glue
- Awl or nail
- Large sewing needle
- String

WHAT YOU DO

1. Enlarge the template on page 141 to 11 x 14 inches (27.9 x 35.6 cm) with the photocopy machine.

2. Trace the template onto the back of the picture you had enlarged, the cereal box, and the colored paper, then cut out the pattern from each.

3. Glue the picture to one side of the cereal box template and the colored paper to the other side.

4. Use the awl to poke a hole through each end of the "petals"

so that when the ends are matched up, the holes line up together.

5. Thread the string through the needle and sew the bottom of the globe together by passing the needle through the holes at each end of the petals. You'll need to fold the petals over each other, and in the process, your globe will begin to take shape. Tie a knot in the string and cut off any excess string.

6. Thread another piece of string through the needle and sew the top of the globe together by passing the needle through the holes in the petal tops. Tie a knot, but leave extra sting so you can hang the globe up. Before you recycle the parts you cut away, remember, that's all the extra stuff that needs to be added to a flat map!

WHERE THE RIVERS FLOW

Here's a question that proves that maps can often influence you in ways you didn't expect.

Which way do rivers flow? You probably answered north to south, except for the Nile. Why do they flow north to south? Perhaps you said because you think rivers should flow from top to bottom. If you look at a map, that would make sense; however, rivers move where there's less resistance, which means they take advantage of gravity. So even though it *feels* right that things should move from north to south or up to down and not the other way around, rivers flow down hills and mountains, not down maps. Do some research and check out all the rivers that actually flow south to north. You'll be surprised by what you find.

THE CENTER OF THE WORLD

Congratulations! Right now you're standing at the center of the world. Pretty cool, eh?! But don't get too excited. Though we're used to seeing the world the way maps present it, there are actually an infinite number of centers of the world. If you live in the United States, your world looks like this:

Or if you're from a tiny island in the Pacific Ocean, your world looks like this:

Not too many neighbors!

If you live at the South Pole, the center of the world looks like this:

When you look at a world map or even a satellite photo of Earth, make a note of what countries are featured in the center, and which ones get cut off on one side and appear again on the other side. Think to yourself, "Hmmm, wonder who made this map?" If your answer is, "It was probably somebody who lives in one of the countries in the center of the map," you're probably right.

A note on these photos: These are computer-generated relief globe images of the Earth showing land and undersea topography. They're from the National Geophysical Data Center.

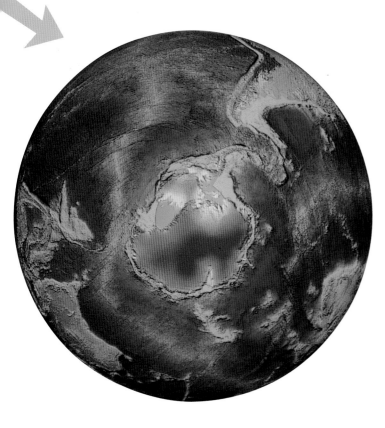

The Flat Map Flap

As you saw on page 45, trying to map something round on a flat piece of paper can be troublesome. Many cartographers have tried and had some success, but something screwy always happens. The cartographer's problem is that you cannot show accurate shape, size, distance, and direction at the same time. Take a look at these four popular world maps *and* what happens to poor old Greenland in each map.

THE MERCATOR PROJECTION

Until recently, this map is the one you've probably seen and worked with. It appeared in most classrooms, atlases, and geography textbooks as a pretty good map of the world. This map was created in 1569 by a cartographer (named Mercator) who wanted to create a map that kept all the directions correct so navigators on ships wouldn't get lost. He decided to create a projection in which direction was represented accurately and the land near the poles would be distorted. So Mercator ended up keeping the continents' shapes accurate while he stretched

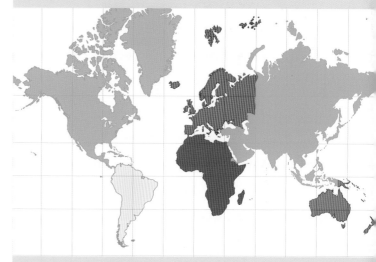

and distorted their sizes. Mercator knew this was going to happen, and though he probably would be proud to have his map in classrooms all over the world, he probably would pitch a fit if he found out that his distortions were not being explained. Most people, after looking at his map, came to believe Greenland was the same size as Africa, even though Africa is 14 times bigger! Plus, the center of the map is western Europe, not the equator.

THE PETERS
PROJECTION

This map, first introduced by cartographer Dr. Arno Peters in 1974, attempts to correct the distortions created by the Mercator Projection. It's called an "equal area map" because it shows all areas according to their actual size (one square inch anywhere on the map equals a constant number of square miles), though their shapes become distorted, making the continents look strange to us. This map is not good for navigating, but it's great for people who want to show all of the areas of the world according to their size and location. It also corrects the perception created by the Mercator projection that the Northern Hemisphere is larger than the Southern Hemisphere.

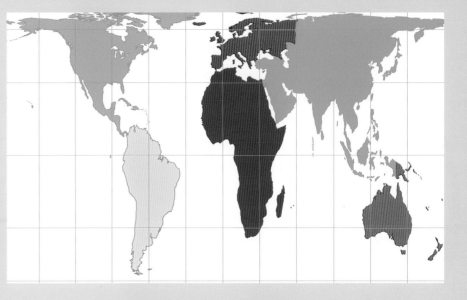

THE ROBINSON
PROJECTION

This map was created in 1963 by cartographer Arthur H. Robinson. It's considered a compromise between other maps. It isn't reliable for navigating, and though it minimizes size and shape distortions, some distortions still exist, especially in the polar regions. Distances are also distorted. This map attempts to show a more accurate picture of the world by distorting size, shape, scale, and area. Sounds like a paradox, but it works.

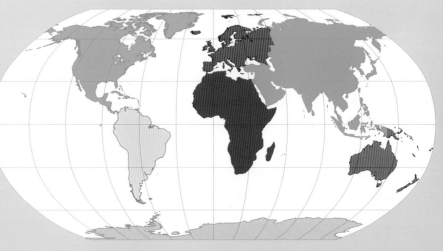

THE WINKEL TRIPEL
PROJECTION

The Winkel Tripel improves on the Robinson projection by distorting the polar areas less to give an even more accurate perspective of the world.

FORGET LATITUDE AND LONGITUDE, GIVE US SOME SEA MONSTERS, UNICORNS, AND MEN WITHOUT NOSES!

Back during that miserable time known to most as the Middle or Dark Ages, before the world had been explored (and much of what had already been discovered about the world had been lost and forgotten), map-

makers had a lot in common with fiction writers. Absurd, you say?! Well, mapmakers back then based most of their maps on pure fantasy. Sometimes they'd draw what little they knew and fill in the empty spaces with doodlings, imagined lands, or whatever came into their heads—none of which had anything to do with rivers, mountains, or cities. Sometimes cartographers didn't know anything about a place and simply drew their maps from stories they overheard, which could include far-fetched tales about sea creatures that swallowed ships whole, mermaids, unicorns, and more! Mapmakers soon found that their colorful, almost entirely unusable, maps sparked people's imaginations and became quite popular. So they kept turning out maps that had less to do with trying to find your way from one

place to another than with entertaining. Many maps from this period were based on the absolutely, positively, unconditionally silly and insane notions put forth by Julius Solinus. His

book, *Gallery of Wonderful Things*, was first published around A.D. 235. In this so-called geography book, he wrote detailed descriptions of places he never visited and people he never met. Some of Solinus's best whoppers include:

• A race of dog-headed people ruled by a dog-king
• People with four eyes
• Ants as big as dogs
• A mule-like creature with an upper lip so long that it must walk backwards in order to eat
• Tribes who had eight-toed feet that were turned backwards
• People with only one leg, but with a foot so large that it protected them from the hot sun by serving as an umbrella
• People with ears so long that they used them as blankets at night
• People with only one eye just above their noses
• People without noses

• And our favorite one of all: people whose eyes and mouths were on their chests

Funny, yes, but unfortunately, some of these stories were considered fact for up to a thousand years. So the next time someone asks you why the Dark Ages were "Dark," tell them about this guy Solinus.

TOPOGRAPHIC MAP OF A FRIEND'S FACE

Topographic maps solve the problem cartographers have when they attempt to show elevation on a flat map. A favorite of hikers, "topo" maps show the height off the ground of hills, valleys, and cliffs using *contour lines* to give the appearance of height.

Contour lines are imaginary lines on the ground that join places of the same height. Think of them as lines that will go anywhere in order to maintain a constant elevation. If the contours are close together, then the slope is steep; if they're spaced wide apart, then the slope is more gentle. If you see hardly any contours at all, then the area is almost flat. For another perspective, think of a region completely underwater in your tub. As you slowly let the water out, the water leaves rings. Those rings are contours.

You can create contours on a map using lines, but nothing says contours quite like face paints!

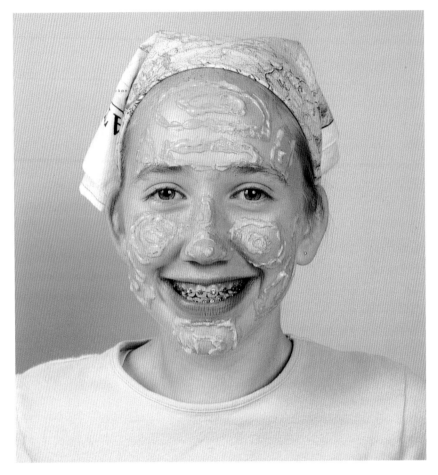

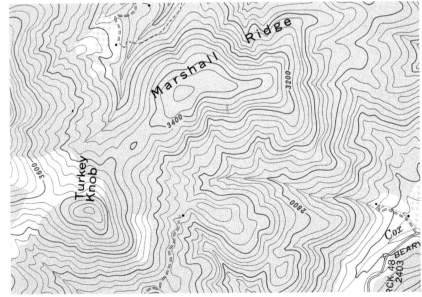

A topographic map

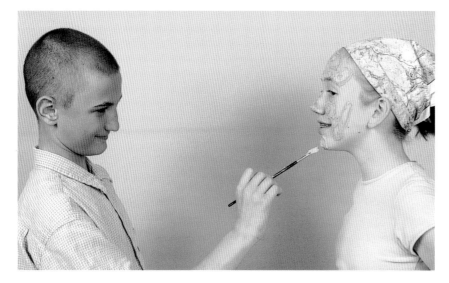

WHAT YOU NEED
- 1 tablespoon (14 g) cornstarch
- 1 1/2 teaspoons (7.5 mL) of water
- 4 1/2 teaspoons (22.5 mL) cold cream
- Bowl
- Spoon
- Food coloring
- Tissue paper

WHAT YOU DO

1. Mix the cornstarch, water, and cold cream in the bowl until smooth. Add a few drops of the food coloring of your choice.

2. Examine the different features on your friend's face. Imagine her nose is like a mountain, her eyes are like valleys, and her eyebrows are like ridges.

3. With your finger or a small paintbrush, mark the highest point on her face. Then move down from there approximately 1/4 inch (6 mm), and trace the highest features at this level. Continue moving down from the highest point on your friend's face in 1/4-inch (6 mm) intervals until you feel you've thoroughly mapped her face.

4. Carefully lay a piece of tissue paper over your friend's face, and press it against her skin so it sticks to all of her contours.

5. In one swift motion, peel the paper off her face and lay it flat on a table to dry.

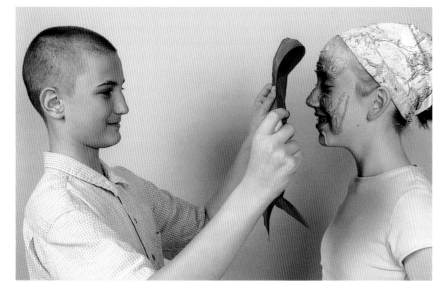

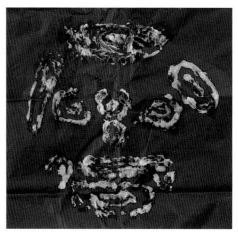

There's Cool, California and Frostproof, Florida. There's Gas, Kansas and Flushing, New York. You may have a good time in Yeehaw Junction, Florida or Celebration, Florida, but don't expect much in Boring, Oregon or Boring, Maryland. Don't get lost in North, South Carolina, and watch where you're walking in Dead Horse, Alaska. There might be some self-esteem problems in Oddville, Kentucky; Odd, West Virginia; Only, Tennessee; Nowhere, Oklahoma; Nameless, Tennessee; and No Name, Colorado. And you may just find the answers to the world's biggest questions in Why, Arizona and Whynot, Mississippi. After visiting Cut and Shoot, Texas, spend some time in Notrees, Texas. Slap Out, Illinois sounds like a good town to skip, though Zook, Kansas and Zap, North Dakota don't sound much better. As for Santa Claus, Indiana; Monkey's Eyebrow, Arizona; Muleshoe, Texas; Experiment, Georgia; and Rough-And-Ready, California; well, let's just say at least they don't have big egos, like the folks in Earth, Texas.

DEEP MAP

A deep map is a map that shows something different. Instead of showing roads, boundaries, and cities far and wide, a deep map goes beneath the surface and tells about what used to be in one place, about the plants and animals that live there, about the people who live there now and who used to live there, about the feel, sounds, and smells of a place. A deep map can be as deep as you want it to be. You might want to tell a lot about the very earliest people who lived there, or you might want to tell where the squirrels that live there now like to congregate. You can also include the geography, natural environment, culture, and spirit of that place and the people who have lived there over time.

WHAT YOU NEED

- Paper for pages, any size you want
- Drawing materials
- Piece of heavy paper for the cover, it should be at least two-and-a-half times as wide as the text pages, and the same height as the text pages
- Ruler
- Scissors
- Small paper clip
- Strong paper clamp
- Awl or nail
- Rubber band, 2 to 3 inches (5.1 to 7.6 cm) long
- Stick, 3 inches (7.6 cm) long, about as thick as a pencil

WHAT YOU DO

1. Begin collecting information about the place you want to deep map. What does the land look like today? What can you find out about the way the land used to look? Go to the library and ask for copies of any maps that include this place. Old maps are especially interesting. Look in old city directories to see who used to live and work in the place years ago. Look in the current directory to see who lives and works there now.

2. Take a walk in the place. What plants grow there? What animals live there? Can you find any animal homes? What kinds of houses and other buildings are there? Talk to the people who live and work there. What can you learn from their stories about the place? What are the special sounds, songs, smells, foods, holidays of this place? Are there any cemeteries? What can you learn about who used to live there? Make drawings and maps of your own, and take notes and photographs.

GEOGRAPHIC BLUNDER: NAMING NOME

Nome, Alaska is probably the best example of a cartographer simply getting it completely wrong. Unlike other cities that are named after founders, heroes, or great cities from the past, Nome, Alaska's name is the direct result of bad handwriting.

In the 1850s, an officer on a British ship off the coast of Alaska noted on a map that a place nearby had no name. He wrote "? Name" next to the point on the map. When the map was recopied, another mapmaker thought that the "?" was a "C" and that the "a" in "Name" was an "o", and thus the mapmaker named the city Cape Nome, which eventually became Nome.

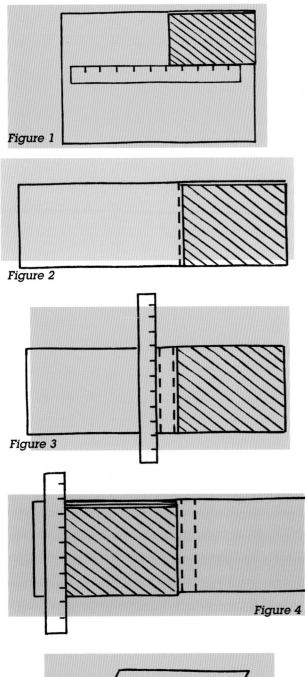

Figure 1

Figure 2

Figure 3

Figure 4

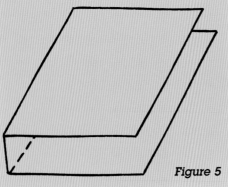

Figure 5

3. When you have lots of information about the place, think about how you want to put it all in the book. Decide how big the pages need to be. What will it take to give a good, deep picture of this special place? Do you need any pages that are extra long and will fold out? Do you need any that have special shapes? Decide which pictures, photographs, or drawings you'd like to include. Write up the stories you want to tell. Make time lines, charts, and diagrams to give other information.

4. Start putting your book together. Don't continue until you know exactly where you want to put everything.

5. Gather all your blank sheets of paper, and write and draw on each page. Be sure to leave a space at least $1^1/_2$ inches (3.8 cm) wide at the left side of each sheet because that's where the binding will be. Assemble all the sheets of paper in the order you want them. Fold in any extra long sheets. Be sure to

include a title page and maybe a blank page at the beginning and at the end of the book.

6. Make a cover for the book out of the heavy paper. To do so, place the stack of pages in one corner of the cover. Place the ruler across the top (figure 1).

7. Remove the stack of pages, but don't move the ruler. Draw a line along the bottom edge of the ruler. Cut the paper along that line.

8. Place the stack of pages at one end of the piece of cover paper that you have just cut (figure 2). Use the small paper clip to score a line on the cover paper along the side of the stack of paper. Remove the stack and use the ruler and paper clip to score another line as far away from the first one as the book is thick (figure 3).

9. Lay the stack of pages on the cover so that its left edge lines up with the second scored line (figure 4). Score along the right edge of the stack. Remove the stack and cut along the line you've just scored. Fold the cover along the other two scored lines as shown in figure 5. Slip the pages into the cover.

10. Tap the book on a tabletop so the pages all line up. Clip the book with the paper clamp along the right edge to hold the pages in place while you bind it (figure 6).

11. Use the awl to poke a hole through the cover and all the pages at one time (figure 6). Keep the awl straight up and down while pressing hard and screwing it back and forth. Poke through from one end, then turn the book over and widen out the hole from the other side.

Figure 6

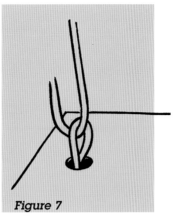

Figure 7

Figure 8

12. Poke this hole around ¹/₂ inch (1.3 cm) down from the top edge and ¹/₂ inch (1.3 cm) from the spine. Poke a second hole ¹/₂ inch (1.3 cm) up from the bottom and ¹/₂ inch (1.3 cm) in from the spine.

13. Unbend the small paper clip; then squeeze a narrow bend or hook in one end. This hook will help

you thread the rubber band through the holes. With the front cover facing you, slip the hook through one of the holes. Put the rubber band on the hook, and pull the hook and rubber band about ¹/₂ inch (1.3 cm) through the hole (figure 7).

14. Slip one end of the stick through

this loop of the rubber band. Now stick the hook through the other hole, and hook the other end of the rubber band. Pull this end through the hole, and slip this loop onto the other end of the stick (figure 8). Decorate the cover to finish your deep map.

Take a Deep Breath and Say...

"Llanfairpwllgwyngyllgogerychwyrndrobwyll-llantysiliogogogoch."

That's the name of a town in North Wales. But if you think that's a cartographer's nightmare, there's a small hill in New Zealand called Taumatawhakatangihangakoauauotamatea-turipukakapikimaungahoronukupokaiwhenuakitanatahu. Hmmm...nice place to visit, but I wouldn't want to pronounce it.

CREATE A FAVORITE NOVEL MAP

What's your favorite book of all time? Where did the story take place? Most likely there's quite a lot of detail about the "where" of the story. See if you can create a map of the book's location. You might be able to map a whole world, part of a city, a small village, or even every house on a block. You might notice some interesting items, but, even more importantly, you might notice things that are missing. Harper Lee's *To Kill a Mockingbird* is one of those books that teachers make you read in school that's actually awesome. And not only is it one of the coolest books around, but the location of the story is very important, and drawing a map actually helps understand the story. All you have to do is read the book and start adding details to your map as you come across them.

MAIL MAP

As we said before, maps can be created to show you just about anything: trade routes, population growth, or even where your mail comes from. In fact, if you take a close look at postmarks and business addresses, you might learn that certain business activities are concentrated in some regions of your country more than others. Perhaps it's due to the physical topography or how highways and railroads are situated.

Collect the mail that arrives at your home for a few weeks, and clip the postmarks and return addresses from the envelopes and backs of catalogs. Plot them on a national map that includes highways and major cities, and see where all that mail is coming from.

WHAT YOU NEED
- National road map
- A large sheet of cardboard to fit behind the map
- Mail
- Tape
- Pushpins
- Scissors
- String

WHAT YOU DO
1. Tape the road map to the large sheet of cardboard, and find a place to hang your map. Keep the pushpins and string near it.

2. Locate your town or city and mark it with a pushpin.

3. As mail arrives at your home (bills, letters, junk mail) cut out the postmarks and return addresses from the envelopes.

4. Pin the postmarks and return addresses to their matching cities on the map, and connect a piece of string between each new pushpin and the pin on your town or city. You've just created a mail map that tells you something you didn't know before: where all that mail is coming from.

RECYCLED MAP SHADE

With the way the world keeps changing, with islands disappearing and countries forming and changing names, maps become outdated rather quickly. That leaves map stores with large supplies of old maps that are probably slated for recycling. With this project, you can salvage an old map and give it a new use as an inspiring view for daydreaming in your room during long homework assignments.

WHAT YOU NEED

- Fabric-lined window shade
- Newspapers or painter's drop cloth
- Acrylic craft paint
- Large paintbrush, 2 or 3 inches (5 to 7.5 cm) wide
- Map to fit the shade
- Ruler
- Pencil
- Decoupage glue
- Water-based varnish
- $1/4$-inch (6 mm) paintbrush

WHAT YOU DO

1. Unroll the window shade on top of a layer of newspapers or a painter's drop cloth. Spread a thin layer of paint across it with the large paintbrush until you've covered the shade. When dry, flip the shade over and paint the back of it.

2. Center the map on the side of the shade that'll face into your room. You can use the ruler to line the map up evenly by measuring the distance between the edge of the shade and the edge of the map in three places on each side. Use the pencil to mark the corners of the map on the window shade. Then set the map aside.

3. With the large paintbrush, spread an even and thin layer of decoupage glue across the shade, keeping inside of the box where the map was centered. Use the marks you made at the corners as guides.

4. Ask a friend to help you carefully lay the map back in place on the shade. Beginning in the center, smooth the map against the shade with your hands. Try to flatten out any air bubbles or creases in the map as you work around it. Some of the glue may soak through the map so that it looks wet or dark in color in some spots. Decoupage glue dries clear, so the color differences should go away once the glue has dried.

5. You may notice some spots along the edges where the map didn't stick to the shade.

Use the small paintbrush to spread a thin layer of glue under these areas, and press the map in place.

6. Spread a thin coat of varnish over the entire map and shade to seal it.

7. Hang your shade, sit back, and admire the new view you just created.

To further decorate your shade, create your very own stamp by cutting out a cardboard or foam shape, gluing it to a square piece of cardboard, and using a foam brush to cover the stamp with ink or paint.

61

Chapter 3
We Are Different; We Are the Same

A PARADOX IS A STATEMENT that seems to be contradictory, or saying opposite things, but is true anyway. The title of this chapter is a paradox because even though it's contradicting itself, there's no better way to describe you and your world neighbors. If you took an imaginary walk down your world block, you'd run into all sorts of people wearing all sorts of clothing and speaking all sorts of languages. Some people might look strange to you. Maybe even weird. And the funny thing is, those people would be looking at you and thinking how weird you look. And what's even funnier is that all of these weird people staring at each other share 99.9 percent of their DNA! That's only one example of this "different sameness" we're talking about here. Geography isn't just a science, it's also a celebration of everything that's different and not so different about the 6 billion and then some inhabitants of Earth, and this chapter explores people (including you), how we live in our different corners (okay, okay, that's just an expression) of the world, what we share in common, how we relate our experiences, and what's important to us.

THE TOOTH RAT?

A custom is another word for a tradition or a practice that people of a particular group or region do. For example, when you were around six years old and lost your first primary tooth, your parents probably told you to put it under your pillow, and a tooth fairy would take it during the night and leave you some cash. Pretty good deal. Too bad you only had 20 primary teeth! Most of your friends had the same cool arrangement. That's a custom. Now, if you lost your tooth somewhere else in the world, a completely different creature

may have taken your tooth, including a rat, mouse, hyena, rabbit, dog, beaver, crow, squirrel, or sparrow. Another popular custom, especially in Africa, is to throw your tooth on the roof. And there's usually no cash involved! You're just making sure a new tooth comes in. If you lived in Central or South America, your mom might make an earring or necklace out of your tooth. Other customs include burying the tooth, throwing it out a window, and placing it in a slipper. Just be glad you didn't lose your teeth in Germany. They don't do anything at all with their teeth. Investigate other cultural differences. How do people around the world celebrate birthdays, New Year's, the seasons? What about coming-of-age celebrations?

"MADE IN..." TREASURE HUNT

Made in China

Made in U.S.A.

Made in China

If you've read the introduction way back on page 9, you already realize that this book has been places. Stop reading for a moment and look around your room. Okay, now keep reading. Chances are your stuff, like this book, has been places you've only dreamed of visiting. In fact, there may be nothing in your room that was actually made in your own hometown or country! So even if you've never stepped foot outside your home your entire life, you've still been influenced by most of the world through your stuff. Check out this "treasure hunt" to see all the cool places your stuff has been (try not to get too jealous).

Made in ?

Made in Korea

Made in Canada

Made in China

Made in Pakistan

Made in U.S.A.

WHAT YOU NEED
- Your room
- World map
- Cardboard (optional)
- Glue (optional)
- Piece of paper
- Pen
- Markers or pushpins

WHAT YOU DO

1. Choose any room in your home as your treasure site.

2. Lay your map flat on a table or other hard surface. If you're using pushpins, first glue the map to a thick piece of cardboard.

3. Pick one area of the room and look for the labels on every object in that area, including clothing, furniture, games, electronic equipment, curtains, shoes, and books. Write down the country the object was "made in" on the piece of paper. Keep score of how many objects came from each country.

4. After you've recorded every object in the area, move on to

the next area in the room and repeat step 3. Continue until you've checked as many objects as possible in the room.

5. If you're using a marker, develop a legend for the number of objects for each country. For example, place a large red dot on countries that contributed 20 or more objects to your room, a smaller blue dot on countries that contributed 15 to 19 objects, an even smaller green dot on countries that contributed 10 to 14 objects, and so on.

6. Did you notice anything unusual about your results? Was anything made in your country? If so, what? Was one type of object (CDs, clothing) made in one country? Did some objects have different parts that were made in different countries? Once you've looked over your results, research the countries your stuff came from and how they make their money.

Made in Japan

Made in China

WORLD SNACKS

Circle the correct words and fill in the blank:

There's nothing better than a nice

cold/hot   plate/bowl   of sticky/crunchy/smooth/tangy/hot/

_____ to satisfy my hunger after a long day at school.

Students worldwide will choose different words to describe their afternoon snacks, but the fact remains that everyone needs a snack when they get home from school. Here is a delicious selection of after-school snacks from around the world. Hit the kitchen and decide which you like best.

OATY BARS (NEW ZEALAND)

WHAT YOU NEED
$1/2$ cup butter or margarine (1 stick)
$1/4$ cup sugar
2 cups rolled oats
Use up to four of the following:
1 tablespoon peanut butter
$1/4$ cup raisins
$1/4$ cup banana chips
$1/4$ cup diced dried apricots
$1/4$ cup diced dried apples
$1/4$ cup chocolate chips
$1/4$ cup shredded coconut

WHAT YOU DO
1. Microwave the butter or margarine in a microwave-safe bowl on high for 1 minute.
2. Add the sugar and oats to the melted butter. Stir in up to 4 of the rest of the ingredients.
3. Press the mixture into a 9 x 9-inch microwave-safe dish. Microwave on high for $3 1/2$ minutes.
4. Cool, then refrigerate at least 30 minutes.
5. Cut into squares. Oaty Bars taste best at room temperature. Makes 16 bars.

WATERMELON SLUSHES (THAILAND)

What You Need
6 ice cubes
2 cups seedless watermelon, cubed
1 tablespoon (15 g) sugar or honey

What You Do
1. Crush the ice cubes in a blender or food processor.

2. Add the watermelon pieces, and blend for about 1 minute until the mixture is slushy.
3. Add the sugar or honey, and blend for 10 seconds. Pour the slush into tall glasses. Serves four.

PAIN AU CHOCOLAT (FRANCE)

WHAT YOU NEED
1 hard roll
Butter, softened (optional)
1 bar of milk chocolate

WHAT YOU DO
1. Slice the roll in half.

2. If using butter, spread it on one half of the roll.

3. Sandwich the chocolate bar between the bread.

4. Heat the sandwich in a toaster oven until the chocolate melts. Serves one.

FIVE-SPICE POPCORN (CHINA)

WHAT YOU NEED
$1/3$ cup popcorn kernels
1 cup chow mein noodles (optional)
$1/2$ cup peanuts
$1/3$ cup peanut oil
2 tablespoons soy sauce
1 teaspoon five-spice powder
$1/2$ teaspoon garlic powder
$1/2$ teaspoon sesame salt or salt
$1/2$ teaspoon ground ginger
$1/4$ teaspoon cayenne pepper
$1/8$ teaspoon sugar

WHAT YOU DO
1. Pop the popcorn kernels according to the instructions on the package.

2. Immediately after popping the popcorn, toss in the chow mein noodles and peanuts.

3. Combine the remaining ingredients in a bowl, and mix thoroughly.

4. Slowly pour the mixture over the popcorn, and mix.

5. Pour the popcorn into a large roasting pan. Heat the popcorn in the oven at 300°F (149°C) for 5 to 10 minutes, stir once.

BEANS AND CHIPS (MEXICO)

WHAT YOU NEED
15-ounce can refried beans
$1/2$ cup shredded cheddar cheese
1 tomato, washed and diced (optional)
$1/4$ cup sour cream (optional)
$1/4$ cup guacamole (optional)
Tortilla chips

WHAT YOU DO
1. Mix the beans and cheese in a microwave-safe container. Microwave on high for 45 seconds. Stir, then microwave for another minute and stir again.

2. If desired, layer the diced tomato, the guacamole, and the sour cream over the bean mixture.

3. To eat, scoop out with the tortilla chips. Serves four to six.

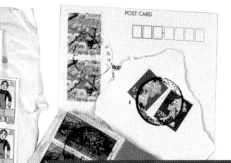

STAMP BOX

If you think a stamp is merely a small piece of paper that tells a postal carrier that you've paid to have a piece of mail delivered, oh how wrong you are! Stamps are tiny windows to the countries of the world.

Pick a country, and collect as many of its stamps as you can. By simply studying a country's stamps you can learn about its history, natural resources, political system, culture, places, citizens, birds, music, theater, dance, science, sports, and more. Many countries put a lot of time and effort into creating beautiful stamps, so that people will buy them and never use them. In fact, creating stamps for collectors is one of the main ways many small countries, such as San Marino (see page 84), make money. Collect stamps from one country or collect stamps from many countries that have the same theme, and turn an ordinary box into a really awesome keepsake box.

WHAT YOU NEED

- Your choice of box
- Paint (optional)
- Small paintbrush
- Stamps
- Decoupage glue
- Craft knife
- Clear acrylic spray paint
- Small hinges with nails
- Hammer
- Decorative trim or upholstery tacks (optional)
- Glue

WHAT YOU DO

1. If your box already has hinges, remove them.

2. Paint the inside of the box, if you wish.

3. Decide how you want to decorate the box, and separate 15 to 20 of your most interesting stamps and set them aside. These will be your final layer on the box, and you don't want to use the coolest ones first.

4. Using the small paintbrush, apply the decoupage glue to the backside of the stamps and place them randomly on the box one at a time.

5. When your box is completely covered, place the lid on the box (without hinges) and apply the favorite stamps, allowing some to overlap the line between the top and bottom of the box. Allow the stamps to dry completely.

6. Find the line between the box and the lid, and press all the way around with your thumbnail. Next, place the craft knife in the groove you made and cut the lid away from the box.

7. Apply two to three coats of decoupage glue to the lid and bottom of the box, allowing each coat to dry thoroughly.

8. Spray the box with two to three coats of clear acrylic spray.

9. Reattach the hinges to the back of the box.

10. Add the decorative trim with the glue, if desired. Fill your box with treasures and enjoy!

FAMILY TREE BATIK BANNER

Who are you? The answers to that question are as varied as the number of people in the world. Many choose to answer this question by stating what nationality they are or what country they live in. Others, however, may state their ethnicity, or what culture or group of people in which their family originated.

Figuring out what your background is can become a fascinating world journey, which means that asking where your parents came from, where their parents came from, where their parents came from, and where their parents came from, until you run out of information, may lead you to many different lands. So, if you need further proof that we live in a global community, trace back your family tree as far as you can. Once you've done your research, "publish" your results on this fabric tree you can hang in your room or give to a relative as a gift.

WHAT YOU NEED

- Paper
- Pencil
- 100% cotton sheet (washed)
- Chalk
- Craft glue
- Paintbrush
- Large piece of cardboard (to fit under the banner)
- Fabric dye
- Salt
- Water
- Spray bottle
- Newspaper
- Rubber gloves
- Wash bin
- Dish soap
- Fusible webbing
- Iron
- 1/4-inch (6 mm) wooden dowel
- Permanent marker

WHAT YOU DO

1. Call your relatives and talk with your parents to get the information you need to draw your family tree on paper. Start with yourself as the trunk, then add two large branches (your parents), then add two branches to each of their branches (your grandparents), and so on as far back as you can trace your history. In doing this, you'll discover that your family has probably moved quite a bit and may even have roots on other continents.

2. Redraw your tree on the fabric with chalk. Leave 1 inch (2.5 cm) around each side of the banner to fold under for a hem later in the project.

3. Use the paintbrush to paint your entire tree with craft glue. Flip the banner over, and paint the tree on this side as well. The glue will block the dye from reaching the fabric wherever it's applied. Lay the banner on the large piece of cardboard, and let the glue dry.

4. Follow the manufacturer's directions, and mix up the dye, salt, and water in the spray bottle. Then, move the cardboard to a spread of newspapers on your driveway or in your yard, and spray the entire banner. You may want to spray the banner several times, as the dye will lighten as it dries and with washing. Let the banner dry before moving to the next step.

5. With rubber gloves on, rinse the banner in a wash tub or metal sink with cold water until the water runs clear from the fabric.

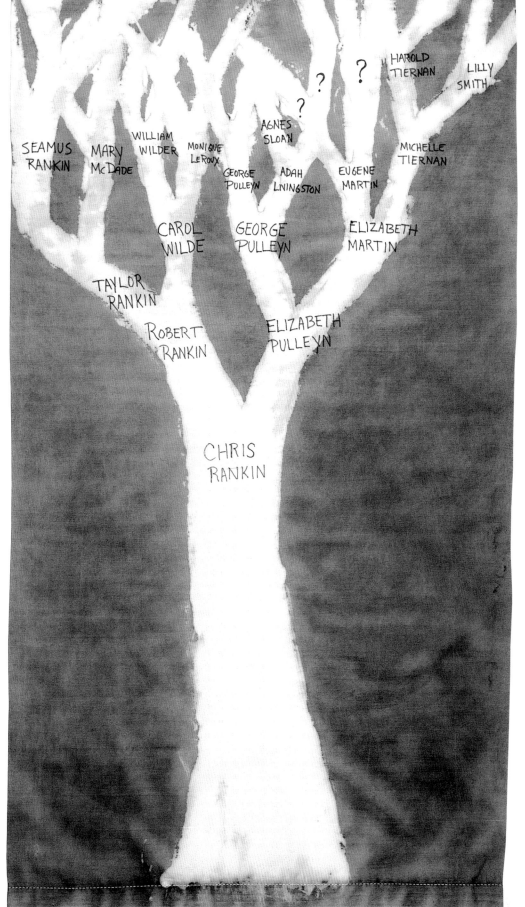

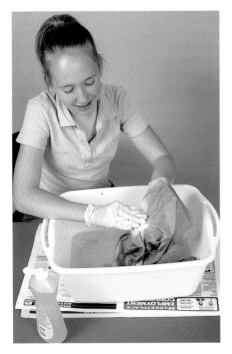

6. Squirt dish soap over the tree design, and in warm water, scrub the glue off the fabric. It should dissolve easily.

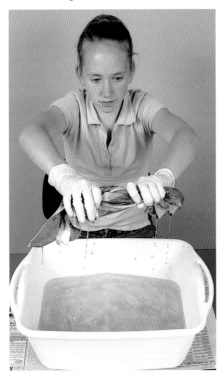

7. Wring out the batik and hang it to dry.

8. Cut four pieces of fusible webbing ¹/₈ inch (3 mm) shorter than each side of the banner. Set your iron to the setting recommended by the fusible webbing manufacturer.

9. Flip the banner so the wrong side faces up, and place a piece of webbing along each side. Fold the sides of the banner over the webbing to make the trim. At the top of the banner, fold enough fabric over to make a pocket for the dowel to slide through above the fusible webbing strip.

10. Press the hot iron against the hems for at least 10 seconds in each spot as you move around the banner. The heat causes the webbing fibers to bind with the sheet to hold the hem in place.

11. Use the permanent marker to write your ancestors' names on the family tree.

Geographers are very interested in the past as well as what's going on today. By studying the past, they can learn about what people thought was important and how that affected how they lived on Earth. You can make tomorrow's geographers' jobs very easy by creating a time capsule that preserves this time in history you're experiencing by including stuff that's important to you and your friends. Or, you can dig it up yourselves years from now, and laugh at the things you thought were important way back then.

WHAT YOU NEED

- Large container with airtight lid
- Paint
- Paintbrushes
- Acid-free tissue paper
- Plastic bags
- Time capsule items
- Shovel

WHAT YOU DO

1. You can use many different containers for your time capsule. Choose something that is made of a nonbiodegradable material, such as plastic or metal. The plastic barrel used here has an airtight lid.

TIME CAPSULE

3. Place each item in a plastic bag to further protect them from rotting (especially paper items).

4. Decorate the capsule.

5. Place the items chosen into the capsule, and seal it.

6. Bury the capsule at least 3 feet (.9 m) underground.

7. Draw a map of the capsule's location (see page 34), and hide it someplace, and if you're going to open it yourself, decide on a date in the future to dig it up.

2. When deciding what to put in your time capsule, think of interesting topics that are important to you, your friends, your community, and your world. Include newspaper headlines, items of social and scientific interest, everyday objects such as a picture of your bike or your parents' car, or even a grocery store receipt. Include mementos of your favorite bands, fashions, and movie stars. Create audio and video tapes. You can even write a letter to the future and tell people what life is like today.

CLAY BOWL

There are some things all humans need to survive: food, water, air, shelter, clothing...but, what about the extras? There are some objects humans have perfected and passed around the world and through generations of people, and no, we're not talking about video games.

Archaeologists, anthropologists, and many geographers learn about past lifestyles based on the ways people decorated and used some of these universal objects, such as baskets, knives, and well...bowls. It may not seem so exciting, but the bowl has a pretty important place on the list of things people around the world choose to have. In other words, just about every ancient culture had cool bowls, and all over the world, people figured out that clay, wood, pounded stone, and woven grasses could be shaped to do something so simple—hold stuff. Mostly they're useful for keeping food together, but at best, they're beautiful pieces of sculpture.

So grab some clay and carry on an ancient tradition, and imagine what someone thousands of years from now would learn about you when they unearth your bowl.

WHAT YOU NEED
- Paper
- Pencil
- Wax paper
- Plastic wrap
- Oven bake clay
- Small bucket of water
- Rolling pin or flat-bottomed pan
- Fork
- Acrylic craft paints
- Paintbrush
- Charms and objects to glue to your finished bowl
- Craft glue or clear-drying, water-based sealant

*available at craft stores

WHAT YOU DO

1. Design your bowl on paper first, and decide how you'll decorate it. Choose symbols or items that are important to you or best describe who and what you are and what you like to do.

2. Cover your work surface with wax paper or plastic wrap.

3. Break off chunks of the clay and work it with your hands to warm it up and make it flexible. Throw it on the table several times, and smoosh it out and squish it back together. When it feels easy to work with, roll the clay into a ball with your hands.

4. Roll the ball on the table to make a long coil. Make a circle with the coil to see how wide your bowl will be. If you want it wider, roll the coil longer. If you want it shorter, cut some clay off the coil. If the clay starts to crack, dip your hands in water and smooth out the cracks with your fingers. You can also spread some water on the clay and then wrap the coil in plastic wrap to absorb the moisture.

5. Make several more coils, wrapping each one in plastic wrap so they don't dry out. The coils should all be the same size so they'll dry evenly.

6. Take a ball of clay and flatten it out with the rolling pin (or use a flat-bottomed pan to press the clay evenly) as wide as you want the base of the bowl to be.

7. Take one of the coils and shape it into a circle. Place it on the clay base, and trim the base to fit the outside edge of the coil.

8. To attach the coil to the base and the coils to each other, use the

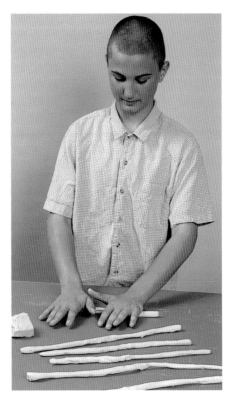

fork to roughen up the sides of the pieces you're going to connect. Pat the roughed-up sides with a little water and then press the pieces together. Smooth the coils together with wet fingers as you move up the bowl. If the clay starts to get dry, wet it with your fingers and let it sit under plastic wrap for a little while to moisten it up. Your finished bowl should be about the same thickness through the walls and the base so it will dry evenly.

9. Use the pencil to make impressions in your finished bowl, and outline the images you want to paint.

10. Follow the clay manufacturer's directions for drying and baking the clay. It's essential that the clay be dry before you bake it or else it'll crack. Small cracks can be patched with some craft glue or covered with paint.

11. Paint your bowl, glue charms onto it, and otherwise decorate it so it becomes an expression of who you are.

12. Seal and protect the inside and outside of the bowl by painting the entire surface with a thin layer of clear-drying craft glue or water-based sealant.

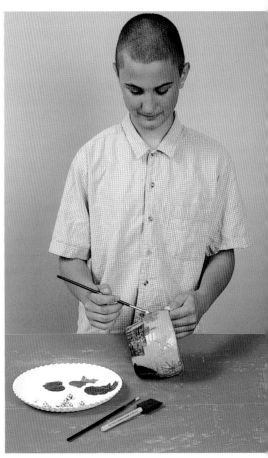

Baa, Moo, Kuk-kurri-kuu

Not only do different cultures see things differently, but they also apparently hear the same things differently. Even something as seemingly easy to "translate" as animal sounds are pronounced differently around the world, even though a cow in Belgium sounds the same as one in China. See if you can match the animal sounds below with the correct animal (answers are at the bottom of the page). Here's a hint: Read the sounds out loud a few times before giving up. The language the sound comes from is in parentheses.

1. Ammuu (Finnish)
2. Ood ood (Thai)
3. Voff (Icelandic)
4. Be-be (Ukrainian)
5. Zoem-zoem (Afrikaans)
6. Cip cip (Italian)
7. Hiihan hiihan (Arabic)
8. Kvakk-kvakk (Norwegian)
9. Berp (Argentinean Spanish)
10. Ake-e-ake-ake (Thai)
11. Choo-hu-hu (Bengali)
12. Ji ji (Mandarin)
13. Qip qip (Albanian)
14. Sss (French) (Okay, some animal sounds are easier than others)
15. Auuuuuuu (Croatian)

Answers: 1. Cow; 2. Pig; 3. Dog; 4. Sheep; 5. Bee; 6. Bird; 7. Donkey; 8. Duck; 9. Frog; 10. Rooster; 11. Horse; 12. Monkey; 13. Mouse; 14. Snake; 15. Wolf

WORLD DRUM

We don't know why, but there's something in our human nature that likes to bang on things. Try passing up a drum in a store without testing it out—it's hard not to at least tap on it. Drums are as old as humans. The oldest drums found so far are from 6,000 B.C.E. and were made from hollowed tree trunks and gourds with animal skins over the top.

Now, what's a drum doing in a geography book? Well, drums, like bowls, appear in almost every culture, without these cultures having had any contact with one another. Drums represent the universal language of music; we may not understand each other's language, but no one can fail to be moved by the sound of a drum. Used in ceremonies as music, speech, or as a healing tool, percussion is the most basic form of music known to humans around the world. Release the ancient rhythm in your hands with this simple-to-make drum.

WHAT YOU NEED

- Cardboard food canister with lid
- Acrylic craft paint
- Paintbrush
- Large, heavy-duty rubber glove
- Scissors
- Elastic band
- Craft knife
- Twine or yarn

WHAT YOU DO

1. Paint the food canister with an even coat of paint, and let it dry.

2. Cut a circle from the wrist portion of the rubber glove so that the rubber circle is approximately 1 inch (2.5 cm) wider in diameter than the canister lid.

3. Stretch the rubber circle across the mouth of the canister so that it's taut, then secure it with the lid rim (figure 1). You can also use an elastic band to hold the rubber circle in place.

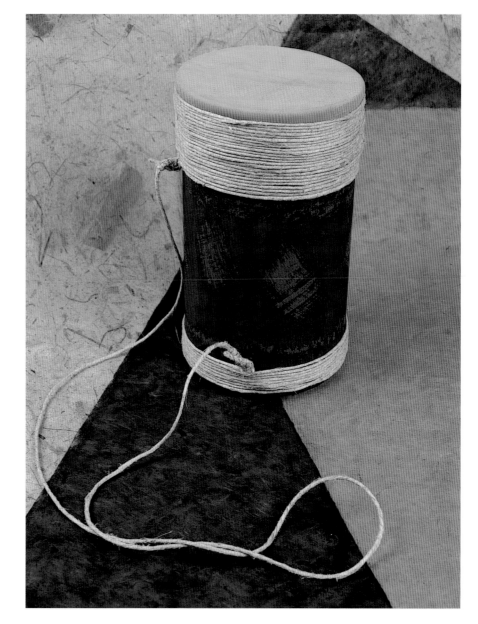

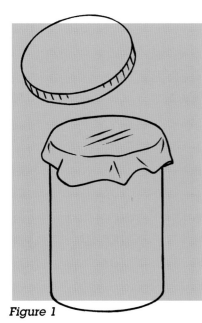

Figure 1

4. Beginning just under the edge of the lid, wrap the twine tightly around the canister until all of the loose rubber is covered (figure 2).

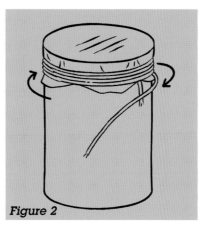

Figure 2

Hold the starting end of the twine diagonally across the can so you can wrap the rest of the twine over it. Tie a knot at the bottom of the wrapped section of the canister. Do the same for the bottom of the canister, but leave enough loose twine so you can use it as a strap for carrying and hanging the drum.

5. Paint the open areas of the drum.

77

FELT STORY CLOTH

Cultures have stories that have been passed down through generations, either through written or spoken word, song, dance, or other ceremony. These stories keep the history of these cultures alive and often teach valuable lessons to those who experience them. One particular culture, the Hmong (see page 80), lost their written language due to years of oppression, and so turned to quilt making to tell their culture's story. These quilts are called "pa ndau" or flower cloths. Create a quilt of your family's journey, and hang it on your wall as a reminder of one of your family's important stories.

WHAT YOU NEED
- Scrap paper and pencil
- Felt squares and pieces
- Scissors
- Fusible webbing
- Iron
- Craft glue
- Paintbrush

WHAT YOU DO

1. Plan out your story. Assign a scene to each square of felt and sketch your idea on paper.

2. Draw the images you want to depict on the felt pieces, and cut them out with scissors.

3. Fit all of the felt squares together so there are no spaces between them.

4. Cut a piece of fusible webbing ¹/₈ inch (3 mm) smaller than the quilt on each side. You'll use this to hold the squares permanently together instead of sewing them to another piece of fabric.

5. Follow the manufacturer's directions for ironing the fusible webbing to the back of the felt squares.

6. Flip the quilt over so the felt squares are on top. Arrange all of the story pieces on the squares.

7. Use the paintbrush to spread the glue evenly on the backs of the story pieces, and glue them in place.

8. Let the quilt dry completely, then share your story without having to say a word.

Fifty percent live within 30 miles (48 km) of the ocean, while over 60 percent live within 100 miles (160 km) of an ocean, sea, or lake.

WHERE YOUR WORLD NEIGHBORS LIVE

Forty-five percent live in cities.

Fifty percent live in Asia, with China and India accounting for nearly two out of every five people on Earth.

Twenty percent live in more developed countries, and less than five percent live in the United States.

People in Motion

If you wanted to know something about your culture's history, you'd go to the library, open up a book, and start reading. But what would you do if your culture had lost its written language? That's exactly what has happened to the Hmong (pronounced "mung"). The Hmong have never had a country of their own and have always been a minority wherever they lived. They called China home for thousands of years until the 1800s, when the Chinese government wanted to change the way they lived. The Hmong refused to give up their culture and left, settling in the mountains of Burma, Laos, Thailand, Cambodia, and Vietnam. It was around this time that they began stitching **pa ndau**, or flower cloths, which are complex and beautiful quilts that show the history, beliefs, culture, and folk art of this proud people.

Three details from a Hmong quilt. See if you can figure out what story is being told in each photo.

The Hmong lived peacefully until the Vietnam War in the 1960s, when, after helping the United States military, they were forced to leave once again. Driven from their homes by hostile governments, they ended up in refugee camps in Thailand. Over 150,000 Hmong have since emigrated to the United States.

By the 1950s, the Hmong written language was lost, and pa ndau became one of the only ways they could retain the stories and customs of the past. Today pa ndau is a cherished art form that relates ancient myths, rituals, past events, as well as more recent events, such as their relocation to America. Each flower cloth is a proud reminder of a strong people's ability to keep their cultural identity alive.

CITIZENSHIP QUIZ

A citizen, national, or subject is a person who owes allegiance to a nation or state and is entitled to the state's protection. Usually, simply having parents who are citizens and the fact that you were born in the country is enough to make you a citizen. Countries have different rules and guidelines for people who live in the country but who are not yet citizens. Often these "aliens" have to live in the country for a period of time. Sometimes there's a test and a lot of paperwork to fill out. There could even be language requirements and documents to get proving you're of good character. Citizenship tests can be quite demanding, asking questions that many of the country's natural-born citizens may not even know. Test yourself and your family to see if you'd pass your own country's citizenship test.

WHAT YOU NEED
- Computer with Internet access
- Paper
- Pen

WHAT YOU DO
1. Go to your favorite Internet browser site and type in "citizenship quiz" and the name of your home country. You'll probably find several sites. Many of them will be sites that list questions to help immi-grants prepare for the citizenship quiz. If you don't have access to the Internet, call your local immigration office and ask for study materials for the test. Some countries have whole books you have to read before tak-ing the test.

2. Write down several of the most interesting questions you find.

3. Type up the questions on your computer, and create a test for your family and friends. Create an answer key for yourself.

4. Give your test and see how many pass. What do your test results say about the citizenship test? How much do citizens of your country know about the history, political system, and culture of your country?

5. Try doing this for other countries as well. Could you pass the citizenship tests given by Japan, Russia, or South Africa? Good luck!

WATCH YOUR WORLD MANNERS, PLEASE

The next time you let out a loud, rumbling belch after dinner, tell your mom (or whoever cooked dinner) that in Saudi Arabia burping after a meal is considered a compliment. The louder the better! Or the next time you slurp your soup, explain that in Japan and Korea that's as good as saying "My compliments to the chef!" Now, you may not get away with this behavior, because your mom's answer will most likely be, "Well, we don't live in Saudi Arabia or Japan or Korea, so stop burping and slurping at the table!"

Manners are important because they help people interact, and if you're visiting another country, you have to be careful because innocent things you would normally do in your own country may offend someone where you're visiting. Here are some examples:

- In Nepal, don't sit with the bottoms of your feet pointing toward others. The soles of your feet are considered unclean.
- If you're sitting on a crowded bus in Zimbabwe (and you're a kid), it's impolite not to offer your seat to an adult.
- Don't chew gum in public in Switzerland. It's considered inappropriate.
- Don't sniff the food in Botswana; nobody will eat it if you do.
- Don't whistle in Tibet.
- Never shake hands or pass food with your left hand in Thailand.
- It's impolite to refuse food in Zambia.
- Using the "thumbs up sign" is considered rude in Bangladesh.
- Don't wink in Hong Kong.
- Long or frequent eye contact is discouraged in Japan.
- Don't hug or pat people's backs in China.

TOP 10 WORLD LANGUAGES

You probably know that Mandarin is the most widely spoken language in the world, but you may be surprised to know that more people speak Mandarin than Spanish and English combined. Here's a list of the top 10 languages according to how many people speak them:
1. Chinese, Mandarin (885 million) 2. Spanish (332 million) 3. English (322 million) 4. Bengal (189 million) 5. Hindi (182 million) 6. Portuguese (170 million) 7. Russian (170 million) 8. Japanese (125 million) 9. German (98 million) 10. Chinese, Wu (77 million)

THE 10 SMALLEST COUNTRIES IN THE WORLD

Imagine if your neighborhood was an entire country. Who would be your ruler? What would your government be? How would relations with your bordering "countries" be? Use the coordinates provided below to find these tiny countries on a world map. Some of these countries really are the size of your neighborhood!

RANK	COUNTRY	AREA	POPULATION	LOCATION (latitude & longitude)
1	Vatican City	0.2 square miles (.5 km^2)	Less than 800	41°54' N, 12°27' E
2	Monaco	0.7 square miles (1.8 km^2)	30,000	43°46 N, 7°23 E
3	Nauru	8.5 square miles (22 km^2)	10,000	1° S, 166° E
4	Tuvalu	9 square miles (23 km^2)	9,700	8° S, 178° E
5	San Marino	24 square miles (62 km^2)	25,000	43°55' N, 12°30' E
6	Liechtenstein	62 square miles (161 km^2)	29,000	47°8' N, 9°35' E
7	Marshall Islands	70 square miles (182 km^2)	52,000	9° N, 171° E
8	St. Kitts and Nevis	104 square miles (270 km^2)	41,000	17°20' N, 62°40' W
9	Seychelles	107 square miles (278 km^2)	69,000	5° S, 56° E
10	Maldives	115 square miles (299 km^2)	181,000	5° N, 73° E

Chapter 4
The Earth Shapes You

THINK ABOUT IT. If the Earth shakes, you shake. And although it's obvious that storms, earthquakes, and other natural phenomena can have a severe impact on our lives, geographers are also fascinated with the not-so-obvious ways in which Earth affects us. Geographers pay close attention to our relationship to Earth and can often tell us why certain towns were built, why a once-booming tourist attraction is now nearly a ghost town, or even how a geological phenomenon that started millions of

years ago affects us to this day. Just because we've explored and mapped most of the world, including ocean floors and mountaintops, doesn't mean geographers are sitting around twiddling their thumbs. They're out there visiting supposedly familiar places and digging up new and amazing information. This relationship between Earth and its dwellers is at the heart of this chapter. Explore weather patterns, how natural landmarks affect your life, why your hometown is where it is, and more by simply turning the page!

WHERE YOU LIVE BROCHURE

How did you end up where you are? Did your parents move to your town, or has your family lived there awhile? Ask your family what drew them to this particular place you now call home.

Great civilizations started out as small groups of people who realized that they had found a good place to call home, whether it was because they had access to a river or the soil was good for planting, or there was good access to other kinds of food. Do some research, call your city leaders, talk to your family, and find out what makes your hometown such a cool place to live, and create a fun brochure advertising your hometown's natural and cultural features that make it distinct and appealing to visitors.

WHAT YOU NEED

- Travel brochures, newspapers, postcards, and photographs from your hometown, plus additional magazines for cutting pictures out
- Scissors
- 11 x 17-inch (27.9 x 43.2 cm) poster paper
- Craft glue
- Foam brush

WHAT YOU DO

1. Take a few minutes to think about what there is to do in your town and surrounding areas. What would be fun to do with a friend who came to visit for a week? Find out why your parents chose to live in your town, and what they like about the area.

2. Go through all of the brochures, magazines, and photographs you've gathered, and cut out images and words that relate to your region. Keep in mind the things you'd want to do with your friend. Look for both man-made attractions (amusement parks, movies, museums) and natural attractions (beaches, scenic views, wildlife) to include in your brochure.

3. Fold the 11 x 17-inch (27.9 x 43.2 cm) piece of poster paper into three equal parts. Then open it back up and lay it down flat in front of you.

4. Arrange the pictures and words on the paper as you like. You may want to overlap images, trim around some of them with the scissors, and leave spaces between others.

5. When you're happy with your arrangement, break out the glue! Working with the bottom layer of images first, use the foam brush to smooth glue over the backs of each image, and press them in place on the poster paper. Continue gluing all the images in place until your brochure is complete. How many of your town's attractions are natural?

6. If you wish, take your finished brochure to a copy center and make several color copies on glossy paper to make your brochure even more appealing. Or with the proper software and some assistance, you can scan your finished brochure into a computer and print a copy on a color printer.

7. Send your brochure to a pen pal or friend to encourage him to visit.

HOMETOWN DETECTIVE

Do you ever wonder about the place where you live? Was it always the way it is now? Where did people go before the mall was built? What was there before the mall was built? When did it all begin? Whether you live in a small town or a section of a big city, some time in the past it was just beginning. Folks came by ship, train, or even covered wagon and created your town. Maybe the old railroad station or the historic water mill is where it began.

If you like detective work and know a little bit about maps, it's a good bet that you may be able to find why your town was built and exactly where it all began.

WHAT YOU NEED
- Journal for note taking
- Camera

WHAT YOU DO
Here are some suggestions on how to get started:

- What natural resources (forests, fish, game, building stone, arable land, etc.) made the location of your town desirable? Chances are some sort of natural resource first attracted settlers to your town. Or perhaps your town grew because it was located between two major cities and became a good resting place. The topographic conditions of your town may have been perfect for a rail line or an airport.
- Did the town grow as natural resources were needed? Did demand for these resources diminish over time, or did your town run out of these resources?

• Most towns start off in a central place like a crossroad or railway depot and spread outward. They usually begin on "Main Street" or a similar name and go from there.

• Take a walk through the oldest part of town (ask your grandparents) and begin to look for clues. Bring along a notebook, and be ready to sketch a homemade map. It's a good idea to bring your camera, too. Be prepared to find old building signs, dates on the tops or cornerstones of the buildings—look for any indications of what kind of business took place there. There may be unusual structures such as storage tanks, silos, and docks. Don't miss the old stone roads, partially covered trolley car tracks, and monuments along the way.

• The names of the streets give wonderful hints to your town's beginnings. First Avenue, Main Street, or Central Boulevard may not be important today, but their names alone tell of past importance. The names of the founders of the town or important historical figures who played a part in the town's history can usually be found on a corner street sign.

• The best part of your investigation is to take your findings to the local library and discuss them with the librarian. Most local libraries are filled with histories, photos, and maps of your town, and the librarian will surely be able to help you.

• There's a good chance other folks are doing the same thing that you're doing, so ask lots of questions and enjoy your search.

Before and After: On September 5, 1996, Hurricane Fran made landfall on the North Carolina coast at Cape Fear. The photo on top was taken before the storm, and the photo below was taken just after the storm.

It used to be that land features influenced where builders put their houses. In other words, you didn't build a town too close to the ocean or a flood plain. With technological advances and incredible population growth, however, people can and do live just about anywhere—at least until nature strikes back.

In developing countries, people are often forced to live in dangerous places such as bare hills where landslides are likely. In other situations, nature is "contained" in order to build. For example, if you want to get closer to a river that tends to flood, you build levees and dams that keep the river from overflowing its banks. And that works fine, until it doesn't work. You see, rivers have this way of continuing to do what they've done for thousands of years.

SALT-DOUGH LANDSCAPE MODEL

To get a good sense of where you live, you need a bird's-eye view to see the bigger picture. From up high you can see population centers clustered together, factories dotting the landscape by the river, desert areas nearly devoid of life, or mountains and hills rising from the ground. Maps often provide you with a good overall view of an area, though even topographic maps don't provide a good three-dimensional look at your town.

With this project you can move mountains, carve valleys, and divert rivers—all with your fingertips. Mix up a batch of dough, and with guidance from a topographic map (page 52), recreate your town's landscape and examine where you live.

WHAT YOU NEED

- Aluminum foil
- 4 cups (560 g) all-purpose flour
- 2 cups (400 g) non-iodized salt
- Large bowl
- Spoon
- 2 cups (.48 L) water
- Topographic map of your area (a map that shows elevations)
- Oven mitts
- Acrylic craft paints, at least three colors
- Paintbrush
- Pencil
- Ice cream sticks, toothpicks, or twigs (for making bridges)

WHAT YOU DO

1. Cover a counter or a tabletop with aluminum foil. (You may need to overlap several sheets of foil to make sure your work surface is completely covered.)

2. Sprinkle a light layer of flour over the foil—this will keep the dough from sticking as you shape it.

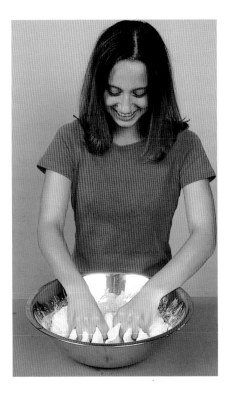

3. Mix the flour and salt together in a large bowl. Slowly add the water while you stir the mixture. Set down your spoon and dig in with your hands. Break up any lumps, and knead the dough until it's smooth.

4. Break off a clump of dough, and work it with your hands until it's warm and easy to shape. Form the handful into a ball, and set it aside on the aluminum foil. Shape the rest of the dough the same way.

5. Examine your topographic map, and plan where you'll need more or less dough to make the land features. Flatten some of the dough balls, and press them together to make the base of your model. The base should be approximately $1/4$ inch (6 mm) thick, but it can be as long and as wide as you want to make it. The model in the picture is 12 x 13 inches (30.5 x 33 cm).

6. Using your topographic map as a guide, add more dough where needed, and shape the model with your fingers to show the most obvious landscape features in your area.

7. To add dough to the model, moisten the piece you want to attach by dipping your finger in water and wiping over it; then press the piece into place. Smooth out the creases and lines where you added the new dough. Continue shaping the model until you can recognize it as your area's landscape.

8. Heat your oven to 250°F (121°C). Carefully set the model with its foil on the center rack.

9. After about two hours, carefully remove the model from the oven. Don't forget to wear oven mitts! At this point, parts of the model will still be wet.

10. Peel the aluminum foil off the bottom of the model.

11. Place the model back in the oven (on the center rack), and bake it until the whole model is dry. It will probably need to bake for a total of four hours. You'll know it's done when you can't make marks in it with your fingernails. It's okay if the bottom's still a little soft.

12. While the model cools, study your topographic map. Notice the places with the most buildings and roads, the areas with only a few houses and roads, and those areas with no roads or houses at all. How does the shape of the landscape affect where people locate? What water features do you see on the map, and what kind of development is around them? What natural features do people seem to be attracted to in your area? What do they avoid?

13. Choose a different color to represent each type of area on your model: one for heavily developed areas (lots of roads and houses), one for lightly developed areas (few roads and houses, some farms and forest), and one for undeveloped areas (no houses or roads). On our model, orange-pink represents heavily developed areas; light green represents lightly developed areas with some houses, roads, farms, and forests; and dark green represents places that haven't been developed. Parks and green spaces are also painted light green. Paint on any water features, such as rivers, lakes, ponds, and marshes. If you live near the ocean, paint an edge of the model to represent the shore. Locate any major roads, especially highways, that cross through your area and paint these on the map as well. To make a bridge, cut a toothpick, ice cream stick, or a thin twig to the size you need, paint it to match the color of your roads, and glue it in place.

PREDICT THE FUTURE!

You don't need a crystal ball to find out how your neighborhood will change in the coming years. Call your local chamber of commerce or town hall, and ask for the latest statistics on population growth and housing development in your area. Examine your model and figure out where you would put the additional people, houses, roads, schools, and businesses, if growth continues. What will happen to parks and the undeveloped areas on your model? How could you add more people without taking up more undeveloped space?

PANGEA PUDDING PUZZLE

Once upon a time (about 4.5 billion years ago) Earth was a big, red fire-ball. As it cooled off some, it rained for a couple thousand years, until all of Earth was one big ocean. Slowly some of the water evaporated, and around 500 million years ago, land chunks emerged and floated around until they came together along the equator, forming one continent that we call *Pangea,* which means "all lands" in Greek. One hundred million years later, the continent began to break up, fractured by shifts in the molten core of the planet. We now have seven continents, which are still shifting, due to *plate tectonics*, the interaction of the moving slabs of rigid rock called plates, which make up Earth's hard shell (see page 95).

Here's a yummy way to travel back to the good old days when you could grow apples in Antarctica and walk to Europe from North America.

WHAT YOU NEED

- 2 large packages of instant pudding
- 1 quart (.95 L) of milk
- Premade cookie dough
- Measuring cup
- Large bowl
- Whisk or fork
- Cookie sheet
- Use of an oven

WHAT YOU DO

1. Combine the pudding ingredients in the bowl, and stir with the fork until it's smooth and thick. Put the pudding in the refrigerator until you're ready to serve it.

2. Flatten the cookie dough out on the cookie sheet until the dough is about ¼ inch (6 mm) thick, and then place it in the oven to bake.

Follow the directions on the dough package for baking times and temperatures.

3. When the cookie dough's done, remove it from the oven. While it's still warm and soft, use a knife to outline the shape of Pangea in the dough (see illustration). Pull the extra cookie from the Pangea outline. Next, draw the fault lines

where the continents we know today tore away from the giant land mass. This time, don't go all the way through the cookie with the knife, but carve about halfway into it.

4. When the dough has completely cooled, slide a knife under it to loosen it from the cookie sheet in one whole piece. Place the giant Pangea cookie on top of the pudding.

5. Dig into the dessert by breaking apart the supercontinent and passing out the new, young landmasses that we float around on today.

Pangea in all its glory! Can you find today's continents in this mess?

SERVING UP SOME PLATE TECTONICS

If you live in California, U.S.A., you're moving to Alaska, whether you like it or not. According to the theory of plate tectonics, California is moving north and will crash into Alaska in around 200 million years. So don't pack your long underwear quite yet.

Earth's crust (outermost layer) isn't a solid shell, but instead, a series of large blocks or plates that drift upon Earth's mantle (first inner layer). According to plate tectonics, these plates are in constant motion, though with an annual speed anywhere from 1/2 to 4 inches (1.3 to 10.2 cm), this isn't something you can feel. These plates may include both oceans and continents, and when they move, the continents and ocean floor above them move as well. Earthquakes and volcanoes are most active where these plates meet, and mountain ranges are formed where plates have collided.

So, what's in store for Earth's continents in the next 100 to 200 million years?

• The Mediterranean Sea may disappear, connecting Africa with Europe.

• India will continue to push into southern Asia, pushing the Himalayas even higher.

• Asia and America may become one continent.

• The Indian Ocean could rise a little and cover the 1,000-plus islands of the Maldives.

• Africa could be split into two continents.

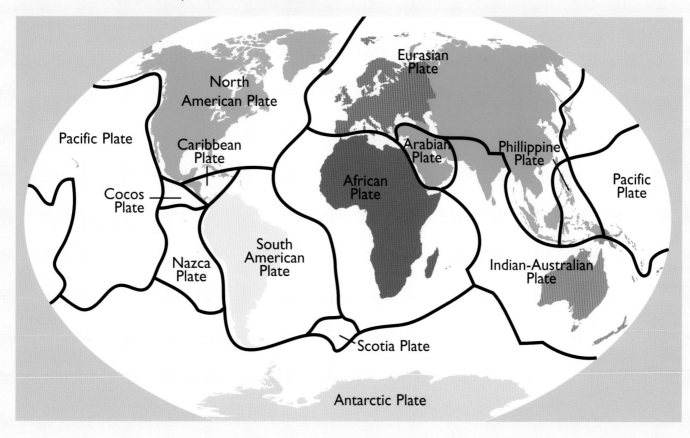

95

CLIMATE STUDY WITH TREE RINGS

Weather is what's happening outside your window right now. Climate, on the other hand, is the overall weather of an area, including average temperatures for months and years, temperature highs and lows, average precipitation, general directions and speeds of winds, and severe weather. And believe it or not, trees are some of the most accurate climate record keepers, able to record evidence of floods, droughts, temperature, lightning strikes, insect attacks, and even earthquakes. How do they do it? If you cut down a tree, you'll notice its growth layers or tree rings—one for each year the tree was alive. The width of each tree ring can tell what conditions were like during that year of growth. The study of tree rings is called **dendrochronology**, and with a tree stump and a ruler you can figure out how the climate changed over the years in your area and compare it to the history of your area.

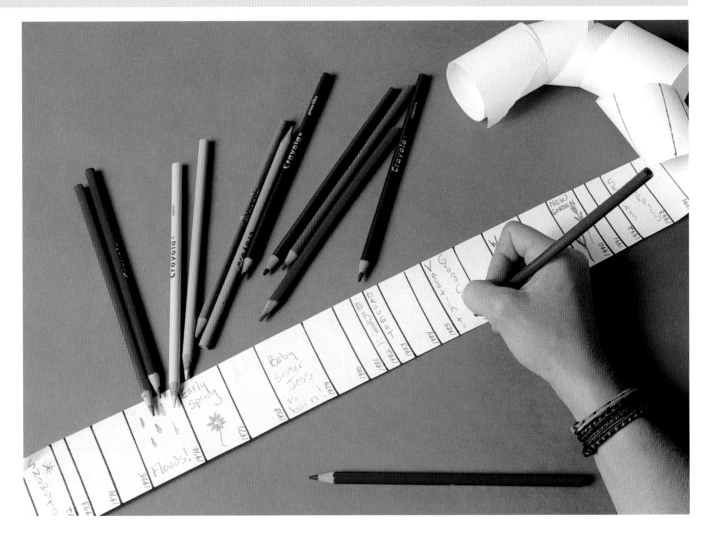

WHAT YOU NEED

- Tree stump in your neighborhood
- Tape measure or ruler
- Journal or piece of paper
- Adding machine tape
- Markers

WHAT YOU DO

1. Find the stump of a tree that has been cut down in your neighborhood. Ask around until you find out what year it was cut down.

2. The outermost ring represents the year the tree was cut down. Measure the width and record the measurement in your journal, along with the year the tree was cut down.

3. List the previous year in your journal and measure the second ring, and so on until you've reached the core. See "Reading Tree Rings" below. When was the tree "born"?

4. Create a time line with the adding machine tape. Record each year the tree was alive from the earliest year to the most recent. Identify years that were good growing years (wide widths) for the tree and those that were poor (narrow widths) by allotting more space on the tape for the good growing years.

5. Ask your parents, grandparents, local librarians, or neighbors about the years on your tape, and fill in each year with information on local weather, history, farming seasons, droughts, and any extreme weather. See if this information matches up with the tree's growing season. For example, your grandparents might recall a three-year drought that corresponds to three consecutive narrow rings. You can

also see if your library has archived copies of your local newspaper. If so, check out the headlines and the weather section for more information. Can you pinpoint specific incidents in your town's history that may have affected the tree's growth?

6. Decorate your time line when you're done.

READING TREE RINGS

- Trees grow from the middle out, so the ring closest to the center is the oldest and the outer rings near the bark are the youngest.
- The dark lines represent the end of growing seasons, and the lighter colored rings represent the actual growing period.
- Wide rings indicate a good growth year, while narrow bands indicate a poor growth year.

WEATHER STATION

Weather can be a pain in the neck. It's always there, threatening your skiing trip or soccer practice or promising one thing and delivering something entirely different—like the predicted GIANT SNOWSTORM that produces only a dusting of snow or the lovely weekend that turns into a swampy, rainy mess. Weather defines where and how you live; it determines what you'll wear and what you'll end up doing. Here's your chance to set up your own weather station and practice the art and science of predicting what kind of weather is heading your way.

WHAT YOU NEED

- Barometer (measures air pressure) (see instructions on page 99)
- Anemometer (measures wind speed) (see instructions on page 101)
- Wind vane (measures wind direction) (see instructions on page 100)
- Thermometer
- Notebook

WHAT YOU DO

1. Once you have made and/or gathered all of your weather instruments, put them in appropriate locations for observing the weather. The wind vane and anemometer should be placed far from buildings and other objects, in an open area. The thermometer should be set up outside, but sheltered from direct sunlight and wind. You can tape it to the inside of a white box (the white will reflect sunlight) and set it on a porch for an accurate reading. The barometer should be set up indoors in a calm area of the house where it won't get knocked over.

2. Set up the pages in your note-book to record each of the following, three times a day: date, time of day, temperature, air pressure, wind direction, wind speed, and cloud type as you have observed them (see page 102 for cloud chart). Plan to observe the weather for at least 14 days or longer.

3. At the end of each day, write your weather prediction for the next day based on your observations. It'll probably take you a few days to get familiar with using your weather instruments, but after two weeks you should have a keen sense of the weather. Wind direction, air pressure, temperature, and cloud cover are basic factors that interact to produce the weather in your region at any given time of day. Careful observation of these factors can forewarn the type of weather that's headed your way. Wind from warmer, wetter regions will bring moisture to your area and may produce precipitation if it meets up with a significantly colder mass of air. Wind from arctic regions will often move in quickly as the colder, denser air mass pushes out the lighter, warmer air mass. Where cold and warm air masses meet, a "front" is produced. Fronts are where all the activity happens as the two air masses struggle with each other—their arrival and intensity announced by the cloud development that accompanies them. The more extreme the difference is between the colliding masses, the more exciting the weather.

Air pressure (measured with a barometer) is the weight of the air on the earth. One square inch (6.5 cm²) column of still air that rises from sea level to the top of the atmosphere weighs 14.7 pounds (6.6 kg)—that's about as heavy as a day's worth of homework packed in your backpack. But the air doesn't just sit in one place over the earth—it's constantly moving. Warm air masses are less dense, and therefore put less pressure on the earth than cold, dense air masses. Tornados, hurricanes, and storms are low-pressure systems. The strong winds that accompany them are caused by air rushing from surrounding high pressure areas to fill the space in the low pressure area. When there's only a slight difference in air pressure between the two masses, you'll measure a gentle breeze with your anemometer, as air calmly moves from areas of high pressure to low pressure. The barometer reflects the degree of pressure being exerted by the air at any given moment. It's one of the fundamental tools meteorologists have used for predicting changes in the weather.

4. Look for patterns in your weather data. What changes seem to go together? Did you notice that wind from a certain direction usually brings rain? What did the cloud formations tell you about incoming weather? Were your weather observations the same or different from the local meteorologist's? If your observations were different from the meteorologist's, what land features and other factors do you suspect influenced the differences?

Making a Barometer

WHAT YOU NEED
- Balloon
- 1 glass jar
- Rubber band
- Drinking straw
- Scissors
- Piece of paper
- Ruler
- Tape
- Pencil

WHAT YOU DO
1. Cut a piece of rubber from the balloon to stretch across the top of the jar. Secure the rubber around the neck of the jar with a rubber band.

2. Snip one end of the straw to make a point. Tape the other end of the straw to the center of the rubber piece that covers the jar.

3. Tape the ruler to the piece of paper lengthwise. Tape the paper to a wall, and place the jar barometer next to it so the pointer is just a hair away from the paper.

4. Three times each day, check the level of the pointer against the paper and make a mark. Use the ruler to compare the distances between the marks. Each time you check the barometer, record where the mark lines up with the ruler.

Making a Wind Vane

(Figure 1)

WHAT YOU NEED

- Thin, long nail
- Drinking straw
- Wood glue

- ⁵/₈ inch-diameter (1.57 cm) metal washer
- ¹/₂ inch-diameter (1.27 cm) wooden dowel, 3 feet (91.4 cm) long
- Hammer
- Scissors
- Index card
- Thin, bendable wire
- Wire cutters
- Compass

WHAT YOU DO

1. Use the scissors to make 1-inch-long (2.5 cm) vertical slits in the top and bottom of one end of the straw.

2. Slip the index card into the slit in the straw, and glue or tape it in place. This end will catch the wind, and the other end of the straw will serve as the pointer.

3. Glue the washer, flat down, to one end of the dowel.

4. Try to balance the straw on your

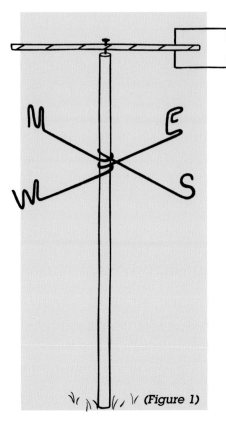

(Figure 1)

finger and pinch the straw where it rests on your finger when you finally get it to balance. Press the nail through the straw where you pinched it, without crushing the straw.

5. Center the nail in the straw over the circle in the washer, and hammer the nail into the dowel. Leave enough of the nail exposed so the straw can spin freely.

6. Hold the dowel vertically, and center the wire horizontally across it, approximately 6 inches (15.2 cm) below the spinner.

7. Wrap the wire around the dowel to hold it in place (this should resemble a cross). Wrap a second piece of wire below the first in the same manner, perpendicular to the first wire. Now you should have four arms of wire extending out from the dowel.

8. Bend the tip of each wire in the shape of a letter for one of the four directions, North, South, East, West. Be sure to follow the order of the directions.

9. Stick the bottom of the dowel in a planter or in the ground, and rotate it as needed so the directions of the wires point in the same directions as the compass.

10. To read the wind direction, just note the direction the pointer end of the weather vane faces. The wind will push the index card away from it, so the pointer end will tell you where the wind is coming from. If the pointer lines up between the direction wires, then record your wind as coming from the northeast, southeast, southwest, or northwest.

Building the Anemometer

(Figure 2)
WHAT YOU NEED

- ³/₄ inch (1.8 cm) x 3 foot (90 cm) piece of wood
- 5¹/₂ x 5¹/₂ inch (13.8 x 13.8 cm) block of wood, ³/₄ inch (1.9 cm) thick
- Hammer
- 2 nails, 1¹/₂ inches (3.8 cm) long
- Pencil or pen
- Scissors
- ⁵/₈-inch (1.6 cm) metal washer
- Wood glue
- 2 pieces of wood trim, ¹/₄ inch x 1 inch x 36 inch (.62 x 2.5 x 90 cm)
- Vegetable oil
- 4 yogurt cups or other plastic cups
- Acrylic craft paint
- Paintbrush
- 4 tacks

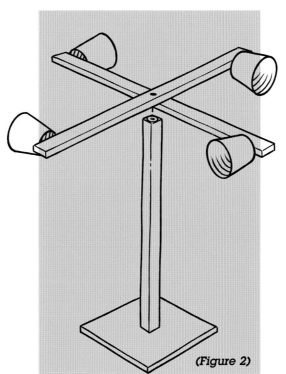

(Figure 2)

WHAT YOU DO

1. Stand the ³/₄ inch (1.8 cm) x 3 foot (90 cm) piece of wood on one end, and center the wood block on top of it. Have an adult help you hammer one of the nails through the center of the block into the end of the piece of wood. This will be the stand for the anemometer. Flip the stand so the wood block is on the ground.

2. Glue the washer, centered, on top of the post.

3. Take the two pieces of wood trim and make a cross. Hammer the remaining nail straight through the hole in the washer and into the top of the post. Leave a ¹/₂ inch of the nail exposed above the post so that the cross-pieces can spin.

4. Give the cross a whirl to see if it spins smoothly. You may want to rub vegetable oil on the washer to reduce friction between the parts.

5. Paint the outside of one of the

yogurt cups with the acrylic paint, and let it dry.

6. Tack the side of a yogurt cup to one of the cross ends, as shown in the illustration. Use glue between the cup and the wood for reinforcement in addition to the tack. Glue and tack the remaining cups to each of the ends of the cross so that the open ends of the cups face the same direction.

MEASURING AND CALCULATING WIND SPEED

1. Ask your partner to time you for one minute as you count the number of times the colored yogurt cup makes a complete circle. Record this number as X revolutions per minute (rpm).

2. Next, find the circumference of the anemometer (the distance around the circle of yogurt cups): circumference = 3.14 (pi) x diameter (the distance across the center of the circle). The circumference calculated for the illustrated anemometer is 56.5 inches (141.3 cm) (3.14 x 18 inches [45 cm] = 56.5 inches [141.3 cm]).

3. Multiply the circumference by the revolutions per minute (X rpm) to get the wind speed in feet (cm) per minute.

4. Convert the wind speed from feet (cm) per minute to miles (km) per hour by multiplying the wind speed by .0114: X ft (cm)/min. (.0114) = X miles (km)/hr.

CLOUD CHART

Many times you can identify the current (or future) weather situation by analysis of cloud type and coverage.

Cumulus prevail during fair, sunny, dry weather.

Stratus are low, dull gray clouds that usually cause overcast skies and steady precipitation.

Nimbostratus are usually the predominant cloud forms during continuous, widespread precipitation.

Cirrus are high clouds that appear feather-like. They are fair-weather clouds and signal the approach of a warm front.

Stratocumulus often appear ominous, but they typically occur during fair weather.

Cumulonimbus are formed when warm, humid air rises and turns to water, which can lead to thunderstorms and tornadoes.

Altocumulus are similar to cumulus clouds, though they are often arranged in lines.

Altostratus form a uniform gray sheet in the sky. Sometimes you can see the sun faintly.

MORE WEATHER FORECASTING TIPS

- Though weather forecasting is a science, sometimes, based on experience, you have a hunch what's going to happen. Follow your hunches.
- Know the climate (highs/lows, average temperature for the time of year, and average rainfall) of your area. This will keep you from predicting a temperature that's 30° lower than the average.
- Once you have a basic understanding of where your weather is coming from, you can note areas that have the same temperature as your region that are experiencing the weather you'll be getting soon and make predictions based on what's happening in those areas.
- Low-pressure areas are probably close to a front and therefore precipitation. High-pressure areas are probably not associated with precipitation. If there's a rapid change in pressure over a short distance, strong winds will result.
- High humidity is usually located ahead of a front, and low humidity is usually behind a front.

RAIN MAP

The movement of the Earth's many plates is not the only way the earth's surface was and continues to be shaped. These great blocks of stone have been chiseled by wind, sunlight, oceans, rivers, and ice. Water may not seem like a good chiseling material, but ice can bust boulders and carve out hollows in mountains. Rain can dissolve limestone, and rivers can cut through a mountain over the course of many years. The next time you look at a topographic map, notice how the rivers have carved out the valleys over thousands of years of traveling through the landscape.

Water also has the power to transform your neighborhood in minutes, when rainstorms send torrents of water rushing down the streets, filling streambeds, and creating puddles. Get outside with this activity and look for signs of the excavating power of water.

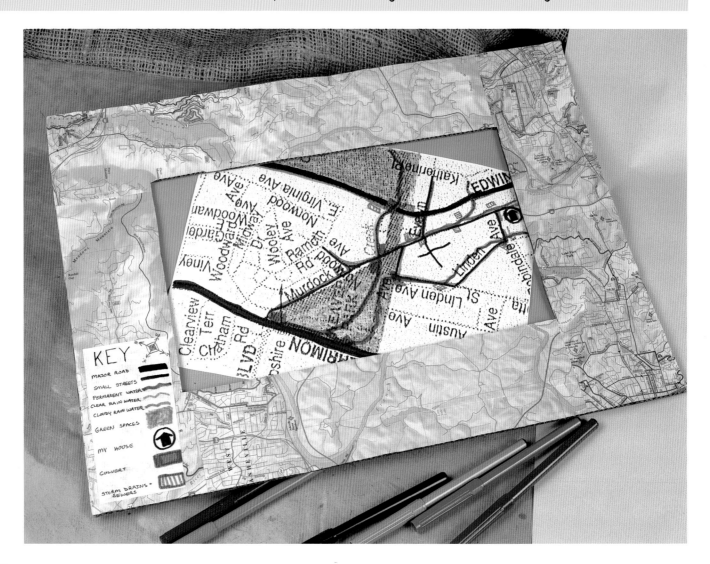

WHAT YOU NEED

- Street map or topographic map
- Use of a photocopy machine
- Clipboard
- Assorted blue, brown, green, and red markers
- 2 pieces of cardboard
- Pencil
- Ruler
- Scissors or craft knife
- Glue
- Paint
- Paintbrush

WHAT YOU DO

1. Enlarge a portion of a street map of your neighborhood so it's large enough to draw in streams and ponds in your area. A topographic map is even better since it already includes some larger water sources.

2. Put your map on the clipboard, and along with your blue, brown, green, and red markers, go for a walk. Look for other sources of water not included on the map. Draw these additional streams or ponds on the map, and use the blue, brown, or green marker, depending on the color of the water you find. Whenever you come across a sewer drain or you notice a water culvert that redirects a stream, draw it on the map with the red marker.

3. Wait for rain.

4. Go back outside with your map and markers right after a rainstorm and look for new sources of water. If you notice that a stream is flooded, use a different color blue to outline the original stream to show that it floods. Draw in puddles and rainwater streams on the streets. Try to match the color of these water features when you draw them. Where does it all go? You've probably noticed that the sky can drop a whole lot of water on your neighborhood, and almost as soon as it appears it starts to disappear. Did you notice too that sewer drains are placed in areas where the water tends to naturally collect because of the Earth's contours and the pull of gravity? These sewer drains lead to a whole network of pipes that eventually release the rainwater into nearby rivers, which in turn pass the water (and all that it carries) into the ocean. Sometimes the rainwater passes through a treatment plant, but more often it goes untreated, and all of the trash and pollutants it picks up in your neighborhood are passed on down the line.

5. Look for *vernal pools*, which are temporary ponds of water that nourish life such as frogs, salamanders, and insects. They appear in the spring when fresh rain raises the water table in the ground to support large puddles in low spots in the terrain. During dry seasons, the water evaporates and the organisms that lived there hop, slither, or slide to new homes. A shallow depression in the ground and dried mud is a clue that there may have once been a pool of life there.

6. To make a frame for your rain map, trace the outside edges of your map onto one of the larger pieces of cardboard.

7. Use the ruler and pencil to measure and mark a 3-inch (7.6 cm) border on the cardboard around the rectangle you just drew, then cut the center rectangle from the cardboard.

8. Paint the second piece of cardboard a color you like as a background for your map. Let it dry.

9. Use a brush to evenly spread glue across the back of your map. Then smooth your map in place on the painted piece of cardboard. Glue the frame on top of this.

10. Cut up a local topographic map to fit the frame, and glue it so the entire frame is covered. Spread a final, thin layer of glue over the frame.

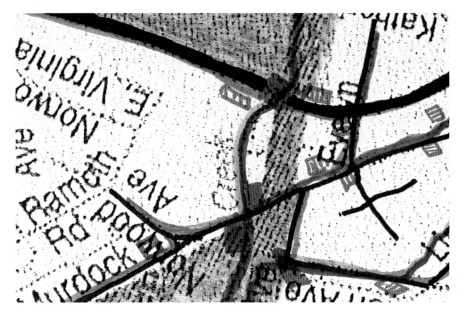

WHAT TRAVELS ON THE WIND

Imagine walking along a dirt road on a windy day when a truck passes by, trailing a cloud of whirling sand, rocks, and dust. The cloud spreads out over the road and slowly dissipates, the dust and other particles settling out wherever the wind took them. Or what if you were to sit near a blooming cherry tree? You would probably find yourself covered with a coat of pollen.

Dirt, pollen, seeds, pollution particles, and anything else light enough to float on the wind can be collected from the air around us and analyzed. But the type and quantity of particles you collect from the air may vary from place to place. Try this activity to find out what the wind carries and how the wind affects what you end up breathing.

WHAT YOU NEED

- 5 rain-free days
- 30 large, white index cards
- Pen
- Nail
- Petroleum jelly
- String
- Scissors
- Notebook
- Plastic wrap
- Magnifying glass

WHAT YOU DO

1. Choose six locations in your neighborhood that have different degrees of development and potential to contribute particles (i.e., dirt, or dust) to the air. For the first three sites, select locations where you expect to accumulate a lot of particles (examples include a heavily used paved road, a parking lot, a gravel/dirt road, a construction site). The last three sites should be places you expect to have the least amount of particles in the air, such as a park, a wooded area, a field, or a backyard.

2. Create six piles of five cards each. Label the cards in each pile with the location where you're going to hang them. If your card has lines on one side, label them on this side. Number the cards in each of the piles from 1 to 5.

3. Carefully punch a hole near one corner of each index card with the nail.

4. Take your cards, notebook, pen, petroleum jelly, string, and scissors to your first location in the morning on the first day.

5. Find a tree branch or other object that is 4 to 6 feet (1.2 to 1.8 m) above the ground.

6. Hang index card 1 for the first

location from the object you've found. Measure the exact distance from the ground to the top of the index card, once you have hung it.

7. Smear a thin layer of petroleum jelly across the blank side of the card.

8. Visit the remaining locations, and hang the remaining number 1 index cards. Make sure the rest of the cards are hung at the same height as the first one you set up, and don't forget to smear the petroleum jelly across the blank sides of these cards as well.

9. At the end of the day, collect the cards from the six sites to ensure that they don't get ruined by dew or a surprise rainstorm overnight.

10. Carefully cover the petroleum jelly side of the cards with a layer of plastic wrap to protect them until the end of the activity. Try to keep the plastic wrap wrinkle free as you wrap it around each card.

11. Record the weather in your notebook, especially noting the amount of wind.

12. Follow steps 6 through 11 for the rest of the days of the activity.

13. After the fifth day, analyze and compare your cards. Look over the cards, and get a general idea of the kinds of particles and matter you collected (dirt, dust, seeds, pollen, etc.). Then, sort the cards from the dirtiest to the cleanest.

14. With help from your magnifying glass, try and figure out just what kinds of particles and matter you collected in each location. Make an educated guess about what activities may have contributed the particles you collected in each location and how far the wind carried them. How did land use relate to the amount and type of particles you collected on the cards? Where would you recommend taking a nap outside in your neighborhood based on air quality?

WHAT IS DUST, ANYWAY?

Dust is just about everything. Think about the dust inside your home. It might be pollen, flakes of skin (our bodies shed nearly half a million flakes of skin per minute), hair, mold, paint particles, carpet fibers, clothes lint, pet dander, bug pieces, dust mites, etc. Outside particles include car emissions, hydrocarbon waste from gas heaters, litter scraps, smokestack particles, tire rubber, soil, pollen, and much, much more! Dust has always been around, but the kind of dust that's been in our air since the Industrial Revolution can be hazardous for anything that needs to breathe.

HOMEMADE BRICKS

Have you ever thought about why homes around the world look radically different from yours? While style has something to do with it, there are two other factors to consider: what's available to build with, and what type of structure will be best for the environmental conditions you're living in. In other words, an igloo isn't such a good idea in the tropics, just as an adobe hut wouldn't be practical in the Arctic.

What's your house made of? If you were suddenly without heat, would you still be comfortable in your home? How practical are the homes in your neighborhood? Does your house have any elements that take advantage of weather conditions? (In Switzerland, the roofs of houses have gentle slopes that allow snow to stay without falling off. This helps insulate the house and keep warm air from escaping.) With this simple recipe, you can make your own bricks to build a miniature house to see how well your materials hold up to the weather.

WHAT YOU NEED
- Topsoil from your yard
- Hardware cloth or a screen with 1/4-inch (6 mm) squares
- 2 large buckets
- Sand
- Tin can
- Water
- Shoe boxes

WHAT YOU DO

1. Sift the topsoil through the hardware cloth and into one bucket to filter out any large rocks or chunks of soil. You want to get a fine soil in the bucket.

2. In the second bucket, mix four cans of the sifted soil with one can of sand.

3. Stir in some water to make a sticky mud. The mud is ready when you can roll it in your hands like clay, without it falling apart.

4. Pack each shoe box full of mud and let them set overnight.

5. Quickly and smoothly, flip each shoe box over to release the mud brick where you want it. If it seems like the brick is going to slump, put the box over it and pack the sides in more. Repeat for each brick.

6. Experiment by adding straw and other natural fibers, shredded bits of plastic, newspaper, and items from your trash to see how they affect the strength and durability of the bricks.

Chapter 5
You Shape the Earth

IN ORDER TO PRESERVE the environment they're exploring, hikers and backpackers live by the rule "leave only footprints." That way the natural environment will still be there for the next visitors. Earth has over 6 billion "hikers," and we're leaving behind some pretty big footprints. Some of these footprints include greenhouse gases, pollution, garbage, enormous parking lots, and malls, all at the expense of Earth's natural resources. Even you alone affect the environment every time you flush the toilet or drink a can of cola. And the only way to explore how we can live lightly on the Earth is to start with ourselves, by looking at what we're doing and how we can do it more responsibly. This chapter explores the ways humans are shaping and changing the Earth and ways we can leave Earth a better place for the next visitors.

SOLAR OVEN

When someone asks to describe a world problem, a common answer is "energy consumption." We are heavily dependent on nonrenewable fossil fuels, and someday we're going to simply run out. And you need an awful lot of energy just to get you through your day. You need electricity to power your alarm clock; gas, oil, or coal to heat the water for your shower; gas to power the car that takes you to school, and so on.

What are some solutions? One answer is right outside your door. Stop reading for a minute and go outside, and you'll instantly feel the power of the sun. Solar technology may be one of the better ways people can produce the energy they need with fewer resources and less pollution. Put it this way, if the sun can transform a couple of pizza boxes and some aluminum foil into an oven, just think of the huge possibilities more advanced solar equipment can offer.

WHAT YOU NEED
- 2 pizza boxes, one larger than the other
- Pencil
- Craft knife
- Aluminum foil
- Newspaper or polystyrene foam
- Nontoxic, black paint
- Paintbrush
- Nontoxic glue
- Sunglasses
- String
- Tape
- Cooking pan
- Piece of clear plastic sheeting that will cover the large pizza box

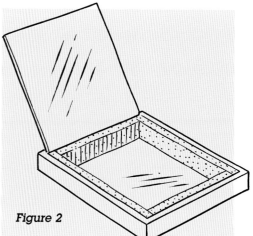

Figure 2

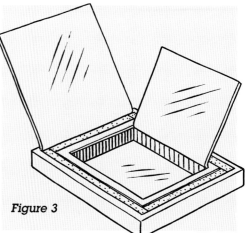

Figure 3

WHAT YOU DO

1. As you work with the solar oven, remember that the point is for it to get hot enough to cook food—in other words, you should treat it like a real oven and exercise some caution when using it. Center the small pizza box on top of the large one with one side touching (figure 1).

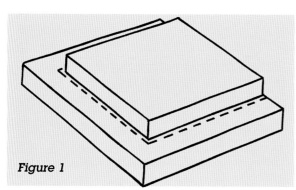

Figure 1

2. Use the pencil to outline all four sides of the smaller pizza box on the lid of the larger box. Set the small box aside and, with the craft knife, cut out three sides of the square you just drew. Leave the fourth side

attached so you still have a connected lid.

3. Line the inside of the large box with aluminum foil, then stuff around the sides with newspaper, or cut polystyrene foam to fill the space (figure 2). This layer of stuffing acts as insulation to help hold the heat in the oven.

4. Fit the small box into the large box, and add more stuffing if needed to fill the space between the two boxes (figure 3).

5. Paint the inside bottom of the small box, and the outside edges of the large box with nontoxic, black paint. Black absorbs heat and will increase the heat in the oven. Line the rest of the box with aluminum foil, and use nontoxic glue to hold it in place.

6. Spread some glue on each of the pizza box flaps, and smooth a large

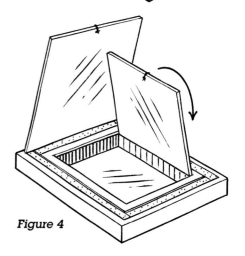

Figure 4

piece of aluminum foil on each (shiny side up). Try to keep the foil as wrinkle free as possible, so sunlight hitting it reflects into the box and doesn't get caught bouncing around wrinkles in the aluminum foil.

7. Adjust the flaps so that they reflect light directly into the box when you line the oven up with the sun. Try not to look directly at the aluminum foil, and wear sunglasses while you adjust the flaps.

8. Poke a hole in the top of each flap, and tie a piece of string through each hole. Tape the other end of each piece of string to the outside of the large box to hold each lid in place at the best angle for reflection (figure 4).

9. Place the food you want to cook on a pan in the oven, and cover the oven with the clear plastic sheeting to trap the heat. Select foods that cook at low to medium temperatures. Cookies, biscuits, pizza, nachos, and other simple foods are perfect for the solar oven. It may take 20 minutes to 2 hours for the food to cook depending on what you're making, so plan ahead and record the baking times for each thing you try.

10. You can use an old cooler as a solar oven by lining it with aluminum foil and painting the inside bottom black. Cover the lid with aluminum foil, and angle it for the best reflection into the cooler. Cover the cooler with a large piece of clear plastic sheeting. Or, use two packing boxes, one large and one small, and fit them together like the pizza boxes. Tear the flaps off the smaller box, but cover the four flaps of the outside box with foil for maximum reflection into the oven.

WATER FILTER

Over one-sixth of the world's population doesn't have access to clean water, due to erosion, pollution, chemical spills, and other environmental disasters, and 80 percent of all diseases in developing countries are transmitted through unsafe water. Boiling water is one way to make water safe to use, but that's not always possible in areas where wood and other fuels are scarce and/or expensive. Desalinating salt water (removing the salt from ocean water) is another possible solution, though at this point it's quite expensive. Other ways are being developed and tested, including using the power of the sun to "pasteurize" water. This project shows you one way water can be filtered, and though this is a cool project, don't use the water from this activity for drinking or cooking.

WHAT YOU NEED

- Small rocks (but too big to fit through the opening of the bottles)
- Sand
- 2 large plastic bottles (2 liter soda bottles work well)
- Scissors
- Charcoal
- Cotton or synthetic stuffing
- Can or pitcher
- Water
- Food coloring
- Spoon
- Strainer

WHAT YOU DO

1. Rinse the rocks, charcoal, and sand to remove dust and residue.

2. Cut the bottom off one of the soda bottles, and cut the neck off the other.

3. Balance the bottomless bottle upside down in the second bottle (see illustration).

4. Fill the bottom third of the top bottle with stuffing, on top of the stuffing add 2 inches (5 cm) of sand, 1 inch (2.5 cm) of charcoal, then fill the rest with rocks.

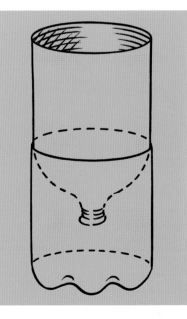

5. Fill the pitcher with water, add a few drops of food coloring, and stir with the spoon.

6. Slowly pour the colored water into the open end of the bottle and watch how it moves through the different layers. Check out the color of the water that collects in the bottom bottle. While we don't recommend you use this to treat water for drinking, you could certainly experiment with using it to treat the "gray water" in your home for reuse to water plants or paint with watercolors. Gray water is the water leftover after washing dishes, brushing your teeth, or doing laundry, that can be reused for other household chores and projects that don't involve drinking or cooking.

❍ Even though Earth is 70 percent water, only 3 percent is fresh water, 2 percent of which is unusable since it's frozen in glaciers and ice sheets. That leaves 1 percent of the world's water supply (much of which is below the earth's surface in natural reservoirs) for plants, animals, and humans to use.

❍ Only .01 percent of fresh water is in the atmosphere at any one time.

❍ Seventy percent of the water used by humans is for farming.

❍ Our bodies are composed of 95 percent water, and the loss of 15 percent of it can be fatal.

❍ 1 quart (.95 L) of oil is enough to contaminate 250,000 gallons (950,000 L) of water.

❍ Americans flush nearly 7 billion gallons (27 billion L) of water down their toilets every day.

❍ The average person in a developed country uses 80 to 100 gallons (304 to 380 L) of water each day.

❍ A large cumulonimbus cloud (see page 103) can hold enough water for 500,000 baths.

❍ If all the water in the atmosphere at any one time was to fall as rain, it would cover the entire Earth's surface to a depth of 1 inch (2.5 cm).

❍ Seventy-five million tons (68 million t) of topsoil is lost to the ocean, either by erosion from wind or water, each year.

❍ It takes around 10 days for a drop of water to evaporate and return to the earth again as rain or snow.

STEPPING STONES

Even our footprints change Earth over time. Animals, like water, seek the shortest and easiest route from one place to another. This applies to humans as well, and many of the ancient animal and human paths have become today's roads and highways. But roads, sidewalks, and other modern "conveniences" don't take shortcuts into account. Take a look around your neighborhood, and watch people walking along the sidewalk. If there's a grass or concrete lot at the corner, do people stay on the sidewalk? No, they cut through the lot. Roads and sidewalks can inhibit these shortcuts, but if you look closely you'll find places where foot traffic has worn away an unexpected path. Create stepping stones with some friends to acknowledge a path naturally carved out by foot traffic near your home or neighborhood.

WHAT YOU NEED

- Sturdy pizza box, or other low box (boxes used for 12-inch [30.5 cm] pizzas work well)
- Clear adhesive shelf paper
- Scissors
- Items for designing the stones: pebbles, shells, baubles, etc.
- Premixed concrete
- Water
- Dust mask
- Rubber gloves
- Mortar box or plastic container
- Hand trowel or hoe
- Piece of plywood
- Plastic bag
- File
- Small, stiff, wire or nylon brush (a toothbrush might work)

WHAT YOU DO

1. These instructions are for one stepping stone. If you're going to make several with your friends, organize your materials and make sure you have enough for everyone before continuing.

2. Look for and map your natural neighborhood paths. Find one that's good for the stepping stone project.

3. Find a good outside location for this project—preferably a place with access to a water hose.

4. Cut a piece of clear adhesive shelf paper to about the size of the inside of the pizza box. Cut the top off the pizza box if you wish.

5. Remove the backing of the shelf paper, and place it in the pizza box with the sticky side up.

6. Create your stepping stone design, making sure that the "face" of each piece in your design is placed facedown onto the sticky shelf paper.

7. Mix the concrete according to the directions on the bag. Wear the dust mask when measuring and pouring the concrete. If you're making a small amount of concrete, you can use a small plastic container and mix it by hand. It's very important that you wear rubber gloves when you do this. If you're working with a bunch of friends, use a mortar box or a wheelbarrow and a trowel or hoe to mix the concrete.

8. Once the concrete is mixed, use a small shovel or the trowel to fill the pizza box with concrete. Do this slowly, and make sure concrete fills in between the pieces of your design. Once all the spaces between the design are filled, add more con-

crete to the box until it's full.

9. Once the pizza box is full, you have to remove air bubbles from the casting. To do this, pick up a corner of the box and tap it up and down against the ground or table where you're working. Use the trowel to level the casting.

10. Allow the casting to remain undisturbed for five to six hours or until the concrete feels firm and no water shows when you rub your finger back and forth over the surface. Take this time to clean up any mess you made.

11. Take the plywood, place it over the casting, and use the plywood to help you turn the casting over. This will help you remove the box without ripping it so you can use it again.

12. Scrub the face of the stone with water and a rag to uncover the parts of the design that the concrete covered up.

13. Cover the stepping stone with the plastic bag, and leave it undisturbed for 24 hours.

14. File the edges of the stone, and use the wire brush to brush away any concrete that's still settled over the design. Wear your gloves and dust mask when you're doing this.

15. Keep the stepping stone wet and covered in plastic for three to five days. This will make the concrete stronger.

16. Your stepping stone is now ready to be placed on the path. Dig out a space for the stones in the dirt so the tops of the stones are level with the ground.

CD MOBILE

As technology changes, so does our garbage. Companies are always on the lookout for faster and cheaper ways to deliver their goods and information. Years ago, milk was delivered in glass containers that were dropped off in front of people's homes. The empty containers were then collected, washed, and used again. Today, you buy milk at grocery stores in cartons made from a specially coated paper that's not easy to recycle, leading to more milk cartons in landfills.

What do you predict will be in your garbage cans in the future? Are there ways to figure out how to recycle these products before they end up in landfills? For this project, you'll be collecting old compact disks (CDs): scratched music CDs or CD-roms, data CDs, or even junk mail CDs, and recycling them into a mobile to brighten up a dreary corner of your room.

WHAT YOU NEED
- Old compact disks
- Fabric paints in squeezable bottles
- Craft glue
- Bamboo sticks or wooden dowels
- Fishing line
- Scissors
- Yarn

WHAT YOU DO

1. Lay the CDs label-side down, so the shimmery side is facing you. Draw your designs on them with the fabric paint. Note: Squeezable fabric paints are fun to use, but it can be tricky drawing and keeping an even pressure on the bottle at the same time. Practice first on a thick piece of paper or old fabric.

2. After the CDs are dry, glue them together, back to back, so that a painted design shows on either side.

3. To prepare the CDs to hang, cut a long piece of fishing line (up to 3 feet [.9 m] long) for each CD. Tie each line through the centers of the CDs. Tie several knots so the lines don't slip, and leave a long tail to hang the CDs to the mobile.

4. You may have an idea of what you want your mobile to look like, or you may have even drawn a picture. If not, now's the time to experiment. How many sticks do you want to use? How many CDs do you wish to hang off each stick? The trickiest thing about making a mobile is *balance*. Be prepared to spend some time making tiny adjustments to the spacing of each CD in order to get the mobile to swing freely and evenly.

5. Tie a piece of fishing line to the main branch of your mobile and hang it from a hook in your ceiling. You may need a stepladder. Hang the other branches to the main

branch so they're balanced.

6. To hang the decorated CDs from each branch, begin tying CDs to the branches, varying the length of the lines. At this point, the mobile will probably sag on one side and not be balanced.

7. Move the CD lines along the branches until the mobile's balanced and you're happy with the design. You may have to add or remove a CD to make the mobile work. Also, use this time to decide if you like where the CDs are located. You may want to shorten some of the lines or take a CD off and give it a longer line.

8. Cut several short pieces of yarn. To secure the lines to the branches, hold a loop in place on the branch, and spread glue on both sides of it, about ¹/₂ inch (1.3 cm) on each side. Wrap the yarn around the branch, beginning on one side of the loop (at the edge of the glue), passing over the fishing line loop and continuing to the other side. Make sure

the yarn is wound tightly since this is what will hold your loops in place. Do this for all the CD and branch strings. You can still make minor adjustments while the glue dries.

TRASH TRIVIA

☛ The world produces up to 1 billion tons (.9 billion t) of solid waste each year.

☛ If we recycle, we can reduce the amount of waste going to landfills and incinerators by 20 to 50 percent.

☛ The United States has 5 percent of the world's population and produces half of the world's garbage.

☛ 17 trees are saved when 1 ton (.9 t) of paper is recycled.

☛ Each American uses about 100 pounds (45 kg) of glass per year.

☛ Almost one-third of the waste generated in developed countries is packaging.

☛ There are over 100,000 pieces of man-made litter in space.

☛ We throw away 2.5 million plastic bottles every hour.

☛ Recycling an aluminum soda can saves 96 percent of the energy used to make a can from ore, and produces 95 percent less air pollution and 97 percent less water pollution.

☛ Over 100,000 marine mammals and over 2 million seabirds die every year by ingesting improperly disposed of plastic.

☛ It takes your trashed paper 2 months to biodegrade; your orange peels, 5 months; milk carton, 6 months; plastic bag, 11 years; shoe, up to 40 years; aluminum can, up to 500 years; polystyrene foam (packing peanuts, etc.), never.

DEBATE BOOK

You hear about the state of the world's environment all the time in the news. Don't you ever wonder why governments and organizations don't just take care of the problems once and for all? The next time you're troubled by a report in the news about the environment or any other world issue, find out more about the issue. You'll probably realize that the problem is a lot more complex than you imagined. Perhaps protecting an endangered animal means restricting access to water a city needs. Or maybe there are people whose lives depend on the grazing land created by cutting down rain forests. This three-part debate book is designed to hold two conflicting points of view on an issue that concerns you, along with possible solutions.

and crease them firmly. Slide them inside each other to make three booklets, one for each section of the book.

4. Fold the long piece of cardboard for the cover into three sections (figure 1).

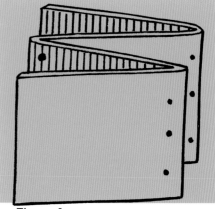

Figure 1

5. Place each signature in position in the cover, and hold them in place with paper clips.

6. Use the awl or sharp nail to poke three holes in the center of each signature and through the cover.

7. Sew the thread into each signature in place as shown in figure 2. Don't tie a knot in the thread. Poke the needle from the outside through the center hole to the inside of the book. Pull the thread through, but

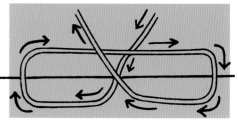

Figure 2

leave about 4 inches (10.2 cm) of string on the outside.

8. Poke the needle through the top hole and out the back of the book,

WHAT YOU NEED

- Pictures, news articles, summaries of information from all sides of your issue
- Several sheets of paper, 6 x 14$\frac{1}{2}$ inches (15.2 x 36.8 cm)
- Piece of corrugated cardboard, 6$\frac{1}{2}$ x 22 inches (16.5 x 55.9 cm)
- Paper clips
- Awl or sharp nail
- Thread or waxed linen
- Large sewing needle
- 6 beads
- Markers, pens, and/or acrylic craft paint
- Scissors or craft knife
- Craft glue
- Foam brush
- Stamps and ink (optional)

WHAT YOU DO

1. Spend some time exploring the issue that has caught your attention. Hit the library, read magazines, or do an Internet search. Collect information from both sides of the issue, and also start thinking about how you'd solve the problem. Remember, learning about the other side of the issue isn't the same as agreeing with it.

2. Sort through the materials you've gathered, and separate them into three piles: one side of the issue, the other side of the issue, and solutions.

3. Fold the 6 x 14$\frac{1}{2}$-inch (15.2 x 36.8 cm) pages in half sideways

then down to the bottom hole and in through to the inside of the book. Poke the needle back into the center hole and out the back. Pull both ends of the thread tight, and make a knot (figure 3).

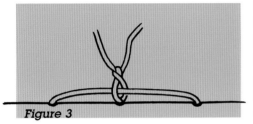

Figure 3

9. Decorate the excess string with beads (tie knots below the beads to keep them in place).

10. Decorate the inside and outside of the cover to make it appealing and to provoke curiosity.

11. Use one section to place your information on one side of the issue. Use the last section to place your information on the other side of the issue. And use the middle to provide solutions you've learned about or thought of on your own. Use a foam brush to smooth glue onto the backs of pictures and information that you plan to stick to the inside pages. Include charts, graphs, statistics, letters to the editor, and whatever else you find that tackles the issue. If you're going to use this book to help others understand the issue, use plenty of colorful images and lots of facts, so people will be drawn to the book and will want to look through it. In your solutions section include information people

could take away with them. Sample letters, names and addresses of related organizations they can join, and tips and advice people can easily act on, are key for empowering others to help out with your effort. Share your book with classmates, family members, friends, and community decision makers. At the very least, you'll learn about something that matters to you, and who knows, you may even inspire a movement.

12. You can make your own stamp to use as a symbol and as decoration on your book. Simply draw a figure on a piece of foam or cardboard. Cut away the excess material, and you've got yourself an image to print with.

TO FISH OR NOT TO FISH: A DEBATE

One world issue that has gotten a lot of attention is what to do about fishing the world's oceans, lakes, and rivers. It's an issue that not only focuses on how our world appetite can affect whole species, but also how attempting to fix a problem can cause more problems.

ONE SIDE OF THE PROBLEM

When you think of fishing, an image of a couple of people on a boat casting lines from their fishing poles may come to mind. However, that's not how most of the world's fish are caught. The majority of the fish you find in supermarkets have been caught by fleets of huge ships that cast out gigantic nets in the deep ocean in order to capture entire schools of tuna and other popular fish. These nets also capture whatever else is in their way. While some nations have laws that discourage taking non-fish species, on the open ocean (which means free from national borders and their laws), fishing fleets are able to act as they desire. The huge nets don't discriminate tuna from dolphins, sea turtles, or wading birds, and by the time the nets are emptied and cleaned, it's usually too late for anything that accidently got tied up in them. This

type of fishing also quickly leads to overfishing, to the point where it would take years for some aquatic life to build up their population numbers again. Overfishing and catching large numbers of fish in nets should be outlawed.

ANOTHER SIDE OF THE PROBLEM

The world demands fish. Fishing has been a way of life for thousands of years, and in some parts of the world, it's the cornerstone of local diets, providing important nutrients for humans. In the United States alone, consumers spend almost $50 billion on seafood. Eating fish has been linked to brain growth in children, heart attack reductions, and a decrease in dyslexia and other learning problems. Also, there are hundreds of thousands of independent fishermen that depend on fishing for their livelihood. Fishing is a hard life, and any and every advantage should be used. By severely limiting how fishing can be done, you're not only denying the world of the fish it needs, but you're also preventing fishermen from making a decent living.

WHAT'S YOUR SOLUTION?

Food for Thought

The Hunger Banquet on page 126 is a modified version of the one created by Oxfam, a nonprofit organization that seeks solutions to hunger, poverty, and social injustice around the world. What does Oxfam suggest you do to help fight world hunger and poverty?

• Teach others about the causes of, and solutions to, these problems.

• Shop wisely; buy only what you need, and get it from socially responsible companies.

• Raise money or volunteer for organizations that work with poor people to improve their lives.

You can find out more about Oxfam by checking out their website, www.oxfamamerica.org, or write to Oxfam, 26 West Street, Boston, MA 02111-1206.

Where's Your Slice?

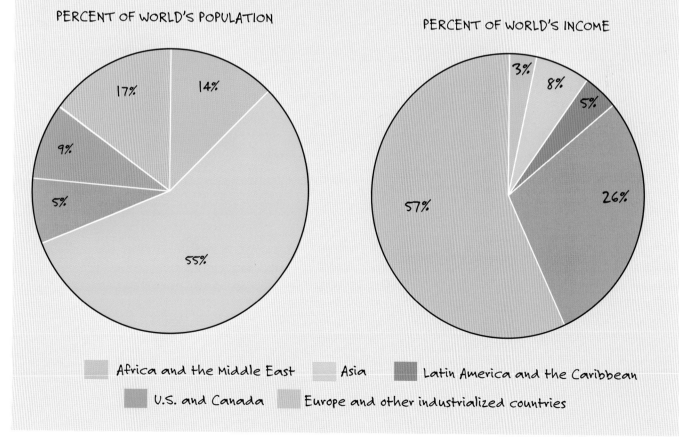

PERCENT OF WORLD'S POPULATION

17% 14% 9% 5% 55%

PERCENT OF WORLD'S INCOME

3% 8% 5% 57% 26%

Africa and the Middle East   Asia   Latin America and the Caribbean

U.S. and Canada   Europe and other industrialized countries

WORLD HUNGER BANQUET

Let's say you and nine friends are going to split an 8-slice pizza. You and one friend go to pick it up. On the way home, you and your friend eat 6 of the slices, leaving 2 slices for your 8 friends. Some friends you are! We don't suggest you try this at home, but let's say this pizza represents all of the world's food and energy. Who do you and your one hungry friend represent? North America, Europe, and parts of South Asia and the Pacific. Who do your other eight friends represent? What's called the developing countries that represent 80 percent of the world's population, including South and Central America, Asia, and Africa. The world's pizza is big enough for everyone, it's just that much of the world doesn't have access to it. Host a hunger banquet with your friends to drive this thought home.

WHAT YOU NEED
- 100 pieces of candy (gum, lollipops, jelly beans, malt balls, etc.)
- 9 friends and yourself
- 5 index cards
- 10 small slips of paper
- A pencil or marker

WHAT YOU DO
1. Write "Africa and the Middle East" on one index card. Write "Asia" on the second card, "Latin America and the Caribbean" on the third, "U.S. and Canada" on the fourth, and "Europe and other industrialized countries" on the last card.
2. Place the index cards around the room, with the "U.S. and Canada" and "Europe and other industrialized countries" at a table, "Latin America and the Caribbean" on a rug or floor pillows, and "Africa and the Middle East" and "Asia" in a small, crowded space.

3. Write "Africa and the Middle East" on one of the small slips of paper, "U.S. and Canada" on another, and "Latin America and the Caribbean" on another. Write "Asia" on five slips, and "Europe and other industrialized countries" on two slips. These slips represent the population of each "continent" as a percentage of the world's total. For example, Asia has about half of the world's total population, so it gets five of the 10 slips.

4. Fold up the slips of paper, and have each guest draw one as they arrive at the banquet. Once they open the slips of paper, have them go to that "continent's" designated area.

5. Distribute the candy to each "continent," telling the guests not to eat it. "Africa and the Middle East" gets three pieces of candy, "Asia" gets eight pieces, "Latin America and the Caribbean" gets five pieces, "U.S. and Canada" gets 26 pieces and "Europe and other industrialized countries" gets 57 pieces. The candy represents the wealth of each "continent" as a percentage of the world's total. For example, "Europe and other industrialized countries" has over half of the world's total wealth.

6. After the candy gets passed out, guests can take turns explaining how they think the candy should be divided. Some guests (most likely the ones with a lot of candy) may not want the distribution to change. Other guests might suggest giving each person an equal amount. Talk about why food and wealth aren't equally distributed around the world. Should that be changed? If so, try to come up with ideas on how to do it.

POPULATION NUMBERS

Though the world's poverty problem is more about access than it is about resources, that may not always be the case, since the more people you have on Earth, the more resources are needed for them to live. Consider this: It took from the beginning of time until 1830 for the world's population to reach 1 billion; the second billion took 100 years; the third billion took 30 years; the fourth billion took 14 years; the fifth billion took 13 years; the sixth billion took 12 years; and unless there's a tremendous effort to slow the population down (birthrates), the next billion will show up in less than 12 years. By the year 2050 there may be over 9 billion people crowding this planet, which will severely strain Earth's already depleted resources. And where will most of these people that will be born in the next decade live? Over 95 percent of this increase in population will take place in the less-developed countries of Africa, Asia, and Latin America.

MORE NUMBERS

- 30 percent of the people living in developing countries live in poverty.
- 70 percent of the world's poor are female.
- 23 percent of the population live on less than $1 a day.
- 2 billion people have no electricity.
- 2.6 billion people lack basic sanitation.
- 1.1 billion people lack adequate housing.

LUMINARY OF EARTH AT NIGHT

If you could get up out of bed one night and travel to the moon and look back at Earth, what do you think you'd see? To tell you the truth, the Earth's surface would look like a bunch of stars. Satellite images, such as the one on pages 130 and 131 help us to better understand where and how we manage to squeeze onto our planet.

Most of the light reflected into space is generated by urban areas where approximately half of the world's population lives and works. But what about those bright lights in Siberia and in the deserts of Africa? Forest fires, natural gas burn off at oil refineries, and major transportation routes like the Trans-Siberian Railroad (which looks like a string of lights across an otherwise dark landscape) all glow at night and look like huge metropolises from space. With this luminary, you can lie on your bed and imagine that you're up in space, circling the dark side of Earth. Where would you want to land?

EARTH FROM SPACE:
A Global Map of City Lights at Night

With this map, it's pretty easy to tell where most of the world's cities are located. This image was pieced together from several satellite shots of the Earth at night. NASA scientists use this map to measure the size of cities and how these cities affect the Earth. Image by Craig Mayhew and Robert Simmon, NASA GSFC; based on data from the Defense Meteorological Satellite Program courtesy Christopher Elvidge, NOAA National Geophysical Data Center

WHAT YOU NEED

- Cardboard cylinder (oatmeal and cocoa containers work great)
- Ruler
- Rag
- Pencil
- Tape measure
- Photocopy of the world map (template on page 141)
- Marker
- Thin, white chalk
- Tape
- Paintbrush
- Dark blue acrylic craft paint
- Pen
- Safety pin, thick sewing needle, and assorted nails
- Scissors or craft knife
- Flashlight

WHAT YOU DO

1. Remove the wrapping from around the cardboard container, and wipe any dust from the surface with a rag.

2. With the ruler and pencil, measure and mark a line around the center of the upright container. This line represents the equator. Wrap the measuring tape around the cylinder to draw the equator line.

3. Measure the circumference of your container with the tape measure. Compare this measurement with the length of the template map, and enlarge or reduce the map as needed with a photocopier. Wrap your photocopied map around the container to make sure it fits.

4. You now need to transfer the map onto the cardboard container. First, outline the continents on the map with a dark marker so that you can see the map when you turn the paper facedown. With the paper facedown, trace the reverse image of continents with the white chalk. If you're right-handed, you should start tracing from the left, and if left-handed you should begin tracing from the right so you don't smear all your hard work across the page with your shirt sleeve.

5. When the chalk outline is complete, match the equator on the map with the equator line on the container, and tape the map to the container so the chalk side is against the cardboard (you'll want to work with the bottom of the container facing up).

6. With the handle end of the paintbrush, rub along the outline of the continents so the chalk makes a print on the cardboard cylinder.

7. Carefully, peel back one corner of the paper to see that the chalk is leaving an outline; if not, you may need to start over.

8. Trace the finished chalk outline on the cardboard container with a pen to make the chalk lines permanent.

9. Use paint or markers to outline the continents and represent oceans and other major bodies of water. Let the paint dry.

10. Compare your cylinder map with the satellite image of the Earth at night (see pages 130 and 131). Use a safety pin or tack to punch through the cardboard to make pinholes in the locations on Earth that match the light spots shown on the satellite image. Can you identify these cities? Can you guess which spots are due to forest or gas fires? Use the large sewing needle or nail to re-punch the cardboard to emphasize the brightest spots on the map.

11. Cut out a circle in the back of the container, near the base, and slide your flashlight inside the hole to illuminate the container. Don't use your map as a lampshade, and don't use a candle.

12. Compare your luminary to a population map. What major population centers are not represented by the nighttime satellite image? What does this comparison tell you about rural versus urban lifestyles in different regions of the world?

Top 25 Largest Cities on Earth

See if you can find these megacities on the Earth-at-Night satellite image on pages 130 and 131. No cheating. Now check how well you did by comparing the satellite image to a world map. How'd you do?

1.	Tokyo, Japan	35 million people
2.	New York, USA	21 million people
3.	Seoul, South Korea	20 million people
4.	Mexico City, Mexico	19 million people
5.	Bombay, India	19 million people
6.	São Paulo, Brazil	19 million people
7.	Osaka, Japan	18 million people
8.	Los Angeles, USA	17 million people
9.	Cairo, Egypt	15 million people
10.	Manila, Philippines	14 million people
11.	Buenos Aires, Argentina	13 million people
12.	Jakarta, Indonesia	13 million people
13.	Moscow, Russia	13 million people
14.	Calcutta, India	13 million people
15.	Delhi, India	12 million people
16.	London, U.K.	12 million people
17.	Shanghai, China	12 million people
18.	Rio de Janeiro, Brazil	11 million people
19.	Karachi, Pakistan	11 million people
20.	Istanbul, Turkey	11 million people
21.	Teheran, Iran	11 million people
22.	Dhaka, Bangladesh	10 million people
23.	Paris, France	10 million people
24.	Chicago, USA	9 million people
25.	Beijing, China	9 million people

NATIVE HABITAT GARDEN

Just as earthquakes can topple bridges and buildings, and tornadoes can tear up houses, so too do humans have the power to destroy the homes of the wildlife that are native to our neighborhoods. What used to live in your neighborhood before the houses were built and the streets paved? What still survives there? Animals play an important role in the natural world, keeping populations of other living things under control. Birds eat insects and mosquitoes, weasels eat birds' eggs, and foxes eat weasels in some ecosystems. But take part of that formula out, and things grow out of proportion. Mosquitoes might take over the world if it weren't for hungry birds, bats, and frogs. So, investigate the plants and animals that would be beneficial to encourage in your backyard and neighborhood. Build shelters, plant the things they like to eat, provide some water, and see what flourishes around you.

WHAT YOU NEED

- Permission from your parents to turn a part of your backyard into a habitat garden
- Nature field guide (see instructions on page 136)
- Toad houses (see instructions on page 137)
- Yard debris
- Ladybug house
- Butterfly house
- Bird Feeder (see instructions on page 137)

WHAT YOU DO

1. Begin by planning out where you're going to put your habitat garden and what wildlife you wish to attract. The activities below are only a few of the hundreds of ideas available for attracting animals and insects. You can do any or all of these activities to get your habitat garden growing!

2. Look into what animals and insects are native to your area, and write down ways to attract them in your field guide. Also research what plants are native to your area, and plant them where you think they'll grow best.

3. Frogs, toads, and salamanders are disappearing at alarming rates around the globe. Habitat destruction, disease, and climate change are all suspects. Encourage a safe place for these sensitive and threatened creatures to live in your yard. Toads and salamanders love moist, dark places so they can hide safely from predators. Provide some shelter for these bug-eating critters in your yard with a few homemade toad houses (see page 137).

4. If you've ever helped with yard work, raking leaves, cutting

branches, pruning shrubs, then you know how much garden debris can pile up. Instead of burning your yard waste or putting it in bags to haul to the dump, create a fort for animals such as field mice, hedgehogs, rabbits, foxes, birds, and other small critters. These animals can be beneficial for controlling rat populations and insects, and they're interesting to watch. Imagine a rabbit hopping through your backyard or a hedgehog munching on dandelion flowers outside your window.

5. Ladybugs are wonderful helpers in your garden or flowerbed. Their favorite food is the green aphid—the same creature that likes to eat and destroy your plants. Invite ladybugs to hang around your yard by providing them with a shelter they can enjoy. You can

buy a ladybug house at most garden centers. Paint it, then place it in a sunny spot off the ground.

6. Butterflies, those beautiful, graceful pollinators of plants, are threatened. They're disappearing as the native and wild plants they depend on disappear, as yards are planted with grass and fields are turned into parking lots. Because butterflies migrate, new buildings or roads anywhere along their route can affect their survival. Imagine going on a trip across country and then discovering that all the grocery stores and restaurants were closed along the way. You could probably figure out a different route to take, but what if it was a day or more off your path? This is the problem many migrating animals face as they fly into familiar feeding and resting areas, only to discover their resting spots have disappeared. Help butterflies out with a butterfly box. Then research local plantings that attract butterflies.

7. Welcome feathered friends to fuel up at a well-stocked birdfeeder in your yard (see page 137). In return, visiting birds will feast on pesky gnats and mosquitoes and help pollinate flowers to support your growing habitat garden.

8. Observe your garden, and note your new wild neighbors you meet in your field guide.

Field Guide

WHAT YOU NEED

- 5¹/₂ x 10-inch (14 x 25.4 cm) sheets of paper
- 6 x 14-inch (15.2 x 35.6 cm) piece of corrugated cardboard
- Thread
- Large sewing needle
- Craft glue
- 1 small envelope with clasp
- Tape
- Leaves
- Paint
- Twine

WHAT YOU DO

1. Line the stack of paper 3 inches (7.6 cm) from one end of the cardboard.

2. Use the binding method shown on page 122 to sew the pages to the cover.

3. Fold the papers in half to expose the rest of the inside of the cover.

4. Glue the envelope to the inside front cover. You may need to cut the envelope to make it fit in the space. Use tape to reseal the envelope where you've cut it.

5. To decorate your nature journal with leaf prints, simply spread a thin layer of paint on a leaf, and press it in place.

6. Keep your journal closed by tying a piece of twine around it.

Toad House

WHAT YOU NEED

- Terra-cotta flowerpot, whole or broken
- Acrylic paints
- Paintbrush
- Small shovel

WHAT YOU DO

1. Wash and dry the flowerpot.

2. Paint your pot until you're happy with it, and let the paint dry.

3. Find a good, shady hiding place, such as under a bush. Use the shovel to dig out a hole big

enough to bury the pot on its side halfway.

4. Make sure the dirt inside the pot is a little wet. Place a few dead leaves and twigs inside too. You'll know when a toad moves in by the way the dirt at the front of the house gets worn down. That's where the toad sits and waits for its dinner to fly by.

Twiggy Bird Feeder

WHAT YOU NEED

- Plastic bottle
- Scissors or craft knife
- Lots of small twigs
- Glue gun and glue sticks
- Bendable wire

WHAT YOU DO

1. Cut the neck off the bottle with the scissors or craft knife.

2. Carve two holes, opposite from each other, 1 inch (2.5 cm) from the bottom of the bottle.

3. Heat up the glue in the glue gun, then drizzle some over a section of the bottle.

4. While the glue on the bottle is still warm, press twigs flat against the bottle and close together. Cover the entire bottle, working in sections around it with the glue and twigs.

5. Poke a stick through the two holes in the bottom so that some of the stick hangs out on both sides of the bottle. These are the perches the birds balance on while they eat from the bottle.

6. Fill your twiggy feeder with birdseed, and hang it somewhere you can see it.

WHAT'S UP WITH ALL THESE RABBITS?

An unwanted visitor is someone who visits and refuses to leave, sort of like a friend who overstays his welcome in your room. In the environment, however, unwanted visitors are also known as eco-invaders or alien species: plants and animals that come from somewhere else (a different country) and are not native to the area. In their natural surroundings, they may be harmless, but they can completely ruin a different environment. Alien plants and animals can disrupt the natural balance, reduce biodiversity, and transmit diseases. And when the aliens have no natural enemies or predators in their new home, they can reproduce at will, creating a population explosion, which can cause a total ecological nightmare.

Here are some examples of alien species that have wreaked havoc around the world:

• Europeans introduced rabbits to Australia in the 1800s so they'd have something to hunt. Unfortunately, rabbits loved their new home, and their population soon grew to half a billion, ruining grasslands and displacing native species. They still cause problems to this day.

• The East Asian long-horned beetle, who entered the United States in wooden crates from its native China, has already devoured thousands of maple trees in Chicago and New York City.

• Non-native plants can sweep through an area, clogging waterways and reducing the amount of land available for farming. The South American water hyacinth has done this in Southeast Asia.

With travel, transportation, and trade becoming easier and easier in this ever-shrinking world, many of these invaders are coming along for the ride, on ships, in wooden crates, and even in luggage. They're one of the biggest causes of biodiversity loss in the world, and though stricter regulations on imported plants and animals will help, as will better inspections of ships and their cargo, this remains a multi-billion dollar problem.

ONE FINAL THOUGHT: THE ULTIMATE WORLD HERITAGE SITE

A UNESCO (United Nations Educational, Scientific, and Cultural Organization) World Heritage Site is a natural or cultural location that has such great value to the world that it's protected against the threat of damage. This means no one can change it around, knock it down, or otherwise mess with it. There are nearly 700 sites around the world, with more added to the list every year. Some sites include the Great Wall of China, the stone circle of Stonehenge (in the U.K), and Grand Canyon National Park in Arizona (U.S.A).

Can you think of a heritage site in your neighborhood? What can you do to help protect it? And here's a thought: Maybe we should just go ahead and declare Earth THE World Heritage Site, with each one of us as site managers. Hey, it can't hurt. We can't help but shape the Earth, but if we

The Great Wall of China. Photo by Thom Gaines

begin walking on it a bit more carefully, leaving lighter footprints, Earth will continue to be a nourishing, flourishing home planet for us and for future generations. We hope you've enjoyed this geographic journey and that it gave you something fun to do as well as something important to think about. Whatever you end up doing on this Earth, please remember that you can always make a difference.

TEMPLATES

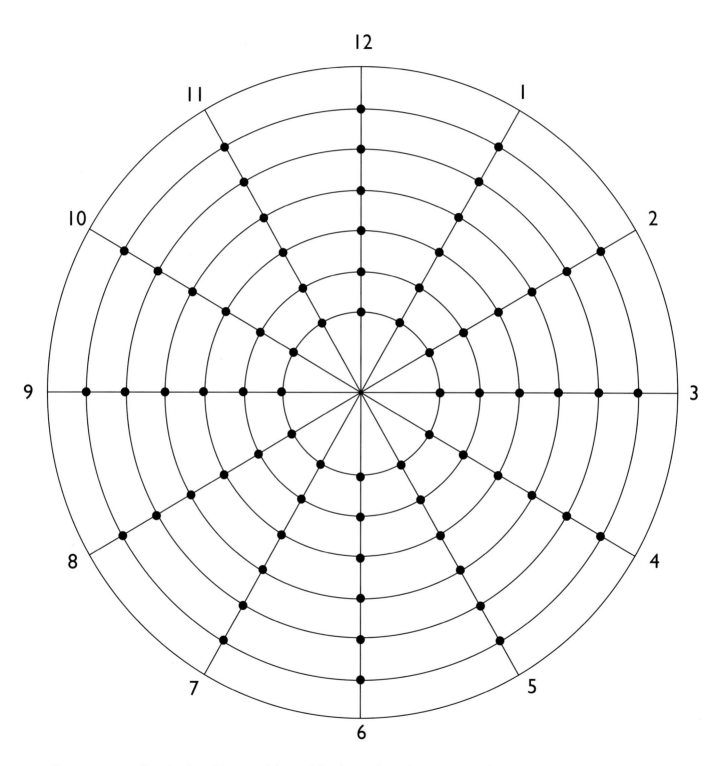

Positioning Guide for Placing Hour Markers for the House Sundial Clock (page 24) and the Time-Zone Clock (page 27)

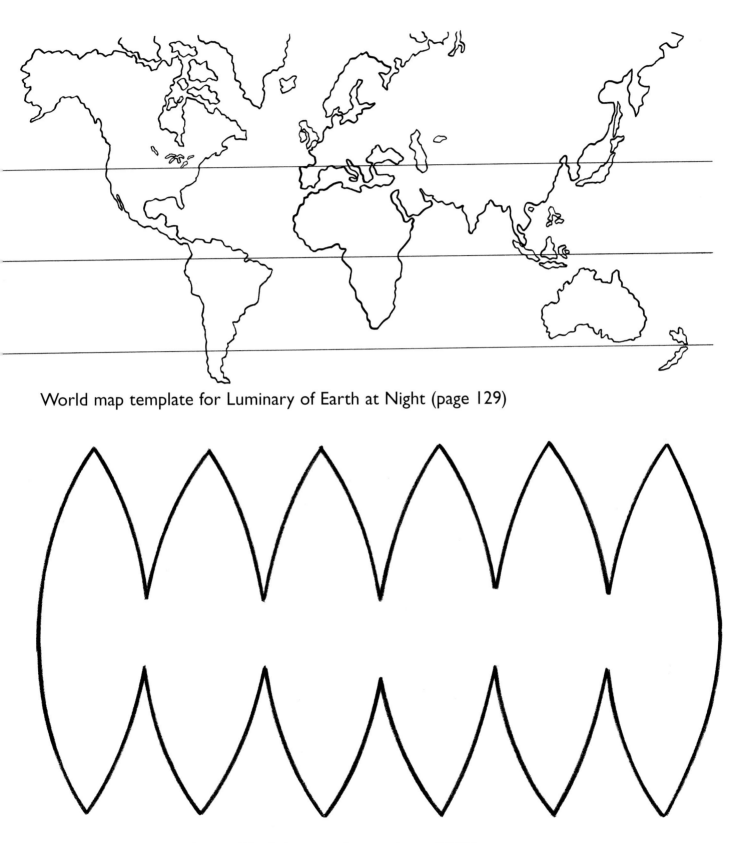

World map template for Luminary of Earth at Night (page 129)

Globe Your Friends (page 45) globe template; enlarge 220%

A NOTE TO EDUCATORS AND PARENTS

Educators around the world have identified several standards or objectives for teaching geography, and we designed the projects in this book with these standards in mind. We've listed the projects under one or more of the objectives we believe the projects help illustrate in order to assist you with using this book as a supplemental aid in teaching geography.

ACKNOWLEDGMENTS

We'd like to thank the following folks for all of their help in creating this cool book:

CELIA NARANJO, for her wonderful design and great spirit (along with her Cool Kid illustrations on pages 57 and 106); Evan Bracken for his excellent photography, as well as for letting us use his GPS receiver and maps; Richard Hasselberg, for finishing the job; Orrin Lundgren, for coming through with some hip illustrations; Joseph M. Rhatigan, for writing his awesome "Hometown Detective" (Hi, Dad!); Nathalie Mornu, super intern, for her great ability at tracking down photographs; Deborah Morgenthal, for her continued support and friendship; Brian Caskey, for hooking us up with software and helping us tremendously with the digital imagery; Veronika Gunter, for always being helpful; Rain Newcomb, for her knowledge of the most random bits of trivia; Carol Taylor and Rob Pulleyn, for expanding their visions of geography; Cindy Burda, for her efforts during the Pangea-stage of this book; and the usual cast of characters at Lark Books

HELEN HOLIFIELD, for creating the CD Mobile on page 118

PAULA HEYES, for creating the lovely Stamp Box on page 68

GWEN DIEHN, for her valuable brainstorming sessions and for the instructions for the Mariner's Astrolabe on page 12, the Cross Staff on page 16, and the Deep Map on page 54

LOUIE MEHLEN, for his project support (woof!)

OUR STUDIO MODELS: Alexandra Fisher, Timothy Christopher McDevitt, Sara Cefalu, Alexandra Nichols, and Dana Detweiler (hey, Dana, thanks for letting us borrow your stuff on pages 64 and 65!); a special thanks goes out to Shannon Rose, for making sure the models got here!

OUR ON-LOCATION MODELS: Marissa Nesbitt, William Ray, Shanbreia Tomes, Steven Martin Payne, Sarah Ruth Payne, Erin Brooke Freeman, Georgia Ann Lawrence, Cody Daniel Griffin, Ian D. Gamble, Donterian Steffon Shivers, Larry Da'shawn Wallace, Patrick Hensley, Tashema Brown, Jazzman Peterson, Thomas Parker Hatley, Kyrisha Jones, and Stephanie Bolden

KATHY HOLMES AND FAMILY, for letting us tramp through their house looking for photo opportunities (Sorry, Jess and Karla, if we left your room a mess!)

ANDREW CAHN AND EMMYE TAFT for providing our Natural Habitat Garden on pages 134-137

BUFFY FOWLER AND DEBBIE RAYMOND at the Francine Delaney New School for Children, for lending us their kids, school, and undying enthusiasm

MARIANNE HAEGI at the Watch and Clock Museum Beyer Zurich; Kelly Talbott and Crissy Robinson at NIST; LaVonda Walton at the U.S. Fish & Wildlife Service;

KATIE RYAN and Sherry Gohl at Library of Congress; Trent Faust, Laura L. Breeden, Omar Patterson, Robert Kratt, and Ramona Traynor at USGS; Jody Russell at NASA Johnson Space Center; Skip Theberge and Robin Warnken at NOAA; Bob Abramms at ODT, Inc.; Dave Knipfer and Donald Larson at Mapping Specialist Limited

THANK YOU, BETH!

PHOTO CREDITS

The What's Up? South! Map on page 33 is available from www.petersmap.com, call toll-free: 1-800-736-1293; More information at www.diversophy.com/maps.htm

The tornado photo on page 85 and the boat photo on page 124 appear courtesy of the NOAA

The Earth images on pages 48 and 49 appear courtesy of the NOAA National Geophysical Data Center

The volcano and earthquake photos on page 85 and the hurricane photos on page 89 appear courtesy of USGS

The photos on pages 6, 8, 10, 12, 17, and 130-131 appear courtesy of NASA

The NIST F-1 photo on page 25 appears courtesy of National Institute of Standards and Technology; photo by Geoffrey Wheeler

Marine chronometer on page 26 appears courtesy of the Clock and Watch Museum Beyer Zurich

The map on page 61 appears courtesy of the U.S. Central Intelligence Agency

OTHER PHOTO CREDITS

Weststock: pages 11, 63, 106, 108

www.comstock.com: page 83 (thumbs up); page 88 (both photos); front cover (compass)

Corbis: page 22 (alien); page 103 (girl in raincoat)

Photodisc: pages 62, 82, 109; rabbit throughout Chapter 5

Image State: pages 92 and 128 (crowd scene); page 139 (footprints);

MediaFocus International, LLC: page 76

Tom Gaines: Great Wall of China, page 139

INDEX